IN SPITE ...˞˞UNS

The Experiences as a Prisoner-of-War in North Korea of the Chaplain to the First Battalion, the Gloucestershire Regiment

In the words of Colonel J. P. Carne, V.C., D.S.O., "This book describes a unique experience. It is a work of significance, and of absorbing human interest." It is a book of faith in adversity and the first detailed account of captivity in Chinese Communist hands. It covers the period from April, 1951, to September, 1953, and is written by the only prisoner-of-war padre who survived the rigours of captivity.

A CROSS FROM KOREA

(*See Appendix I*)

Photo: "*Gloucester Citizen*"

IN SPITE OF DUNGEONS

The Experience as a Prisoner-of-War in
North Korea of the Chaplain to the First
Battalion, the Gloucestershire Regiment

by

S.J. Davies, M.B.E., M.A.

With a Commendation by

General Sir John Hackett

With a Foreword by

Colonel J.P. Carne, V.C., D.S.O., D.L.

ALAN SUTTON

*Parts of this book were originally published
as articles in* The Church Times.

First published November 1954
Second Impression December 1954
Third Impression March 1955
First paperback edition 1957

This edition first published in 1976 by
Alan Sutton Publishing Limited · Phoenix Mill · Far Thrupp
Stroud · Gloucestershire

First published in The United States of America in 1992 by
Alan Sutton Publishing Inc. · 83 Washington Street · Dover · NH 03820

Reprinted in 1978
Reprinted in 1982
Reprinted in 1992

A British Library Cataloguing in Publication Data
record for this book is available.

ISBN 0 7509 0298 1

Library of Congress Cataloguing in Publication Data applied for

Printed in Great Britain
by The Bath Press,
Bath, Avon.

DEDICATED

TO

THE MEN WHO DIED ALONG

THE IMJIN,

AND

AS PRISONERS-OF-WAR IN NORTH KOREA

THE CHAPLAINS OF THE CAPTIVITY

REV. KENNETH L. HYSLOP, chaplain, U.S. Army.
Died in captivity, North Korea, December 10, 1950.

REV. FATHER EMIL J. KAPAUN, chaplain, U.S. Army.
Died in captivity, North Korea, May 23, 1951.

REV. WAYNE H. BURDUE, chaplain, U.S. Army.
Died in captivity, North Korea, July 28, 1951.

REV. S. J. DAVIES, Royal Army Chaplains' Department.
Taken prisoner April 25, 1951. Released September 5,
1953.

COMMENDATION

FROM

GENERAL SIR JOHN HACKETT

The combination of high courage and deep spiritual conviction is, even in defeat, unconquerable. Millions of the world's inhabitants have been taught for half a century and more that only material values endure. Witting tools and what Lenin called 'useful fools', outside the grey, totalitarian prison of Marxist-Leninist dictatorship — even in our own open societies — endorse this view. But whatever happens truth and humanity will in the final sum prevail, and material values, for all their short-lived attraction, and for all the smart dialectic of their sponsors, will be seen to be of less weight than courage and truth and the confidence that these, in the end, will win.

This book by a well-loved army chaplain, now in service as a parish priest in Gloucestershire, 'In Spite of Dungeons', by S.J. Davies, lends powerful support to this conviction, in a document sometimes almost unbearably moving.

Coberley Mill,
May, 1982.

FOREWORD

BY

COLONEL J. P. CARNE, V.C., D.S.O., D.L.

I am very glad to write a foreword to this new edition of a book which though it has been out of print for some years remains a significant work of absorbing human interest.

We of The Gloucestershire Regiment have just commemorated the twenty fifth anniversary of the Battle of Solma-Ri, on the Imjin River, and it is fitting that this book by our old Padre, for so we still think of him, should re-appear at this time.

The book tells of the survival, both spiritual and physical, of prisoners-of-war in Chinese hands in North Korea under a regime of Communist indoctrination, and it is still as relevant now as it was when it was first published to an understanding of the tragic divisions of our modern world. For the author this was his "parish behind barbed wire" in which his services and ministry brought great spiritual comfort.

It is a great satisfaction to his many friends in the Regiment that he is now Rector of Uley here in Gloucestershire, and thus we remain in touch with our Padre of those days.

Cranham,
August, 1976.

PREFACE TO THE 1992 EDITION

It is a happy timing for me that the publisher's decision to issue this new edition happens to coincide with the fiftieth anniversary of my ordination in December this year.

Although the world-scene has changed vastly since our Korean imprisonment, 1951–53, it cannot perhaps be assumed that Communist China has changed so radically. I believe I am the only Service chaplain who has experienced captivity in Chinese Communist hands and undergone the indoctrination process, and it may therefore be conceded that the book is still relevant to an understanding of China's outlook.

What will, I think, always be found relevant is the way in which in my "parish behind barbed wire", and indeed beyond it, the Faith was able to sustain, strengthen and comfort us in an evironment hostile to all Christian belief, and to the best ideals our country had nurtured in us.

This new paperback edition is identical with that of 1982. Colonel Carne, VC, DSO, died on 19 April, 1986. I gave the Address at his funeral at Cranham on 25 April. I retired from my united benefice of Uley cum Owlpen and Nympsfield, Gloucestershire in November 1984, and am privileged to continue my ministry as a non-beneficed priest in the Diocese of Exeter and as Honorary Chaplain to The Gloucestershire Regiment.

S.J. DAVIES
October, 1992.

ACKNOWLEDGMENTS

Major Guy Ward, T.D., R.A., who as a prisoner-of-war in North Korea shared with me so many unusual experiences, most kindly placed at my disposal the originals of his sketches, done behind barbed-wire, of life in P.O.W. Camp 2. I was often grateful in those days for the companionship of one whom Gunners will rejoice to know we christened as Senior Officer, in North Korea, of the Royal Regiment—"C.R.A.N.K."* The inclusion in this book of seven of his sketches gives me further reason for gratitude.

I also wish to thank Major Martin O'Geary, of The Buffs, for his photograph of the hymn from the prisoners' hymn-book, "Faith of our fathers, living still, In spite of dungeon, fire and sword."

I gratefully acknowledge the permission given by the Editor of *The Times* to print my letter originally published in the newspaper on November 20, 1953.

S. J. D.

* Commander, Royal Artillery, North Korea.

CONTENTS

page

TO THE READER 13

chapter

I GLOUCESTER HILL 15

2 IN CHINESE HANDS 28

3 SIX STRANGE MONTHS 35

4 NORTH TO THE YALU 48

5 THE PRISONERS OF PI-CHONG-NI . . . 57

6 THE LENIENT POLICY 71

7 CHURCH OF THE CAPTIVITY: MY PARISH BEHIND
BARBED WIRE 80

8 A GATHERING STORM 93

9 THE SPIDER'S WEB 104

10 IN SPITE OF DUNGEONS 115

11 THE FINAL PHASE 129

12 YU-TI 142

APPENDIX I. "A CROSS FROM KOREA" . . 151

APPENDIX II. A BOOK OF SELECTED PRAYERS . 154

APPENDIX III. A CHRISTMAS SERMON IN PRISON . 156

LIST OF ILLUSTRATIONS

A Cross from Korea . . . . *frontispiece*

FIG.   FACING PAGE

1 The author conducting service at the front, for
   men of the Gloucesters, a few days before the Imjin
   battle began   14

2 An altar for Holy Communion set up in a ruined
   temple in "A" Coy's. village, some six hours before
   the massed Chinese assault across the Imjin River   14

3 Aerial view of Prisoner-of-War Camp 2, Pi-chong-
   ni, North Korea, showing No. 1 Company
   Compound (YF 138018) and, as from October
   16th, 1952, No. 2 Company Compound (YF
   129023)   56

4 Our Chalice, a Chinese soldier's tin mug. It was
   used for the five celebrations of Holy Communion
   the Chinese permitted us in two and a half years'
   captivity   56

5 The wooden Communion Paten carved by Major
   Ryan, inscribed "Behold, the Bread of Angels" .   56

6 A general rear view of Camp 2, from the "House
   on the Hill" (where the senior officers lived until
   October 16th, 1952)   64

7 The "House on the Hill", Camp 2. Here the
   senior officers lived until the camp was split into
   two compounds   64

8 Prisoners' sleeping and general living quarters,
   Camp 2   80

9 The Camp Kitchen, Camp 2. Food was prepared
   here for more than 300 officers and sergeants .   80

10 A Baptismal Certificate on Chinese cigarette-
   paper   84

LIST OF ILLUSTRATIONS

11 The Pagoda 92

12 The carved wooden cover of the hymn-book made
by prisoners in Camp 2, and presented to me at
Easter, 1953 104

13 The scrap of Chinese toilet-paper containing in
rough code the dates and material from which this
book has been written. It was smuggled out of
captivity. Readers are referred to the first paragraph of chapter eight 104

14 The Presentation Hymnal opened at the hymn
sung at the conclusion of every service in the
Prison-Camp, and which epitomized our faith, and
resistance to subversion "In Spite of Dungeons" . 120

15 The beautifully printed and illuminated prayer-
book made in No. 2 Company of P.O.W. Camp 2,
and presented by the prisoners to Captain James
Majury, of the Royal Ulster Rifles . . . 120

16 Presentation page of the Hymnal carved and hand-
printed by prisoners in Camp 2. . . . 128

17 Church Service, March 1953 136

18 Prisoners at Volley-Ball, Camp 2 . . . 136

19 My Communion Paten, lost during the Battle of
the Imjin. Its story is inscribed round the rim (by
Boodle and Dunthorne, the Silversmiths, at
Liverpool) 136

20 The Cross from Korea is handed over to the Dean
for safe-keeping in Gloucester Cathedral, at the
Gloucesters' great Thanksgiving Service, November 21st, 1953 144

TO THE READER

This is the story of life, from the chaplain's point of view, in conditions of captivity by Chinese Communists, and more especially in the officers' compound at Prisoner-of-War Camp No. 2, at Pi-chong-ni in North Korea.

It is a fantastic story, not without its humorous side. I have tried to write it dispassionately, without exaggeration. For much of it there are many witnesses, British and American. Of those instances where my word alone will have to be taken, I should like to say two things.

First, I am the only chaplain to survive of the four military chaplains captured in Korea. This in itself makes me want to speak truly about what I experienced as a prisoner of the Chinese Communists. Secondly, the incidents related, and the dialogue recorded, impressed themselves on my memory like engraving on steel. They are unforgettable. I wish to write the truth, but without rancour, and without vindictiveness or hatred towards the Chinese people.

I believe the book will show something of the resilience of men's spirits under physical and mental pressure of a kind not hitherto experienced by British and American prisoners-of-war. To this resilience, Christian faith made a big contribution. Many men were grateful for its inspiration in a Communist prison-camp.

At the close of our religious gatherings, we used to sing the hymn:

"Faith of our fathers, living still
In spite of dungeon, fire and sword:
O how our hearts beat high with joy,
Whene'er we hear that glorious word:
Faith of our fathers, holy faith,
We will be true to thee till death."

It not only affirmed our faith, but seemed to symbolize our resistance, as men in prison, to calculated attempts at subversion by our captors. That is why I have called my book *In Spite of Dungeons.*

Before capture, it was my privilege to serve the 1st Battalion the Gloucestershire Regiment as chaplain. By their heroic stand at the Imjin River from April 22 to April 25, 1951, the Gloucesters took the brunt of the Chinese attack on the hinge of the western front. By incredible tenacity and self-sacrifice, the hopelessly out-numbered battalion gave Command a vital breathing-space. The great onrush of the enemy's spring offensive was stemmed, and Seoul was not taken.

Of this great feat of arms, which earned the President-ial citation of the United States, his late Majesty King George VI said that it had "Maintained the highest traditions of my fighting services", and had been "justly acclaimed throughout the world". For many who took part in the battle the outcome was captivity.

I have felt it right to devote the first chapter to an impression of the events which occurred on "Gloucester Hill".

In June this year I re-visited the Republic of Korea as a guest of the Korean War Veterans' Association, and was greatly impressed by the achievement and resolute spirit of the South Koreans in face of the continuing threat of invasion from the Communist North. I was very conscious of the indebtedness they feel to the nations who came to their aid twenty six years ago.

Once again I stood on "Gloucester Hill", deeply moved to find the Solma-Ri Memorial — the work of The Royal Sussex Regiment in 1957, assisted by 24 Field Engineer Regiment and 28 Korean Infantry Division — so meticulously and reverently maintained by the Koreans. A guard of two soldiers is continuously mounted, and teams of school children regularly tend the Memorial's surrounds and flower-plots. I was grateful for this opportunity to lay a wreath of freshly cut flowers in remembrance of many old comrades who fell in battle in Korea in defence of freedom, or who died later in the prison-camps.

This book is dedicated to them.

S. J. DAVIES.

Uley,
August, 1976.

1. The author conducting service at the front, for men of the Gloucesters, a few days before the Imjin battle began.

2. An altar for Holy Communion set up in a ruined temple in "A" Company's village, Solma-Ri, some six hours before the massed Chinese assault across the Imjin River.

1. It is a fairly warm spring morning. Along the front the troops are watching and waiting. Some are able to gather for church service in a sheltered hollow.

In the background, a group of officers are assembled at the Command vehicle awaiting instructions from the Adjutant.

The Gloucester officers on the extreme left of the picture are Captain Lutyens-Humfrey (taken prisoner); Captain Pike (taken prisoner); Captain Reeve-Tucker (killed in the Imjin Battle) and Lieutenant Guy Temple (taken prisoner, and later awarded the Military Cross).

Most of the soldiers seen here were captured.

(War Office photo)

2. The board, on which is affixed a crucifix, is leaning against my army chaplain's field communion-case. The candles and chalice, which is covered with a square linen pall, can be seen. In the background, beyond the altar-table, is the ornate gateway to the temple.

The time is 12.30 p.m. on Sunday, April 22nd, 1951. By nightfall all this ground, the location of "A" Coy., was swept by small-arms and mortar fire.

From this altar, two very gallant young officers of "A" Coy. received their last Holy Communion. They were Lieutenant Philip Curtis, killed early on April 23rd and posthumously awarded the V.C.; and Lieutenant Terence Waters, the only officer to survive the night's fighting, who died later in the year as a prisoner-of-war in North Korean hands rather than betray the cause of the United Nations by taking part in propaganda work. He was posthumously awarded the George Cross.

CHAPTER ONE

Gloucester Hill

TWILIGHT was falling on the Imjin River, bring-
ing the grey, chilly April evening to a close. The last of
the returning "Centurions" lurched across the shallows
like gigantic beetles, their antennæ waving. All day, from
crack of dawn, they had probed deep into the "no man's
land" across the Imjin, carrying with them a strong task
force of Gloucesters. There had been desultory firing,
and the infantry had swarmed without opposition across
several trenched slopes. No contact was made with the
Chinese. Everywhere naïvely-worded leaflets were found
urging the United Nations' troops to give up the fight,
and telling them this was a war for the blood-soaked
profits of Morgan, Dupont and Rockefeller. Safe conduct
was guaranteed to those who surrendered in possession
of the leaflet.

It was good to be back on "our side" of the Imjin;
good to sip steaming cocoa in the candlelight, and fall
asleep with the comforting knowledge that the Chinese
Communist forces were miles away beyond the broad
river. The date was Friday, April 20, 1951.

The Fifth Fusiliers lay along the Imjin almost five
miles to the Gloucesters' right flank. Lieutenant-Colonel
Kingsley Foster had invited me to conduct and preach at
their annual Saint George's Day Service, which was
brought forward to Sunday, April 22. The service was

held in the open, at the foot of a steep hill. It was a clear, bracing morning. The strong, manly singing rose courageously into the blue. At the end, the Colonel proudly read the awards for service in Korea recently conferred on members of the battalion by His Majesty. Afterwards we strolled to his tent for sherry. Two days later, the Colonel lay dead in his jeep, riddled with bullets, while the Chinese advance rolled on.

At mid-day I returned to my own battalion, the Gloucesters. I set up my altar in a half-ruined temple in "A" Company's lines, overlooking the Imjin, and celebrated Holy Communion. Among the communicants able to attend were two young subalterns, Terry Waters and Phil Curtis. It was their Viaticum. That very night "A", the Gloucesters' most forward company, was completely enveloped by the Chinese and subjected to a murderous assault. The Commander was killed. Philip Curtis proved an inspiration to his men. Early in the morning he, too, was killed, making a desperate, lone assault, already wounded, against a Chinese machine-gun bunker. The Victoria Cross was conferred upon him posthumously in November, 1953. Among his last acts on earth was the reception of the Blessed Sacrament at my hands.

Terry was the only officer to survive. He got back with the remnants of the Company to Battalion Headquarters on the Monday morning. He died later in the year as a prisoner-of-war in the notorious "Caves", near Pyong-yang, having gallantly resisted all attempts by his North Korean captors to make him take part in propaganda work. In April, 1954, he was posthumously awarded the George Cross. Terry was faced with the choice: "death or dishonour". He chose death.

Chatting and drinking tea together after the service, such endings to their young lives were unimaginable. As we stood in the sunny temple courtyard, word came that a Gloucester patrol across the Imjin was in contact with Chinese troops. The news caused no alarm; we received it carelessly. I bade them good-bye and returned by jeep to Headquarters.

That Sunday evening after nightfall, Guy, the lieutenant in command of the watching patrol at the river-crossing, came back with his men. He was tense and excited. "At first," he said, "it looked like ten or twenty coming across. We killed quite a few. Then I reckon hundreds of them were pouring across in the moonlight."

All around the vast, black humps of the mountains seemed full of menace and foreboding. As I thought of "A" Company lying in front of us in their positions overlooking the river, my stomach turned. The first staccato bursts of firing could be heard. The night came alive with the wicked chatter of small-arms a mile down the road. In bright moonlight the Chinese pushed up the long spur beyond "A" Company, and began to attack "D". All companies became embroiled. Heavy fighting continued throughout the night in the high ground surrounding Battalion Headquarters. Friday's tank probe across the Imjin had revealed little: the enemy had evidently melted away only to surge swiftly forward under cover of darkness. As dawn broke, Mr. Hobbs, the regimental sergeant-major, said to me over a cup of char:

"They'll give up at dawn. Mark my words, sir, they'll go back across the river."

A few minutes later we went to ground as snipers' bullets whined overhead. Then silence.

The blessed light of day came: Saint George's Day, Monday, April 23. Carriers with Lieutenant Cabral in command, set off down the road to extricate the survivors and wounded of "A" Company. Firing had well-nigh ceased and the Chinese, fearing American air activity, had gone to ground. The men of "Able" came in. They had taken terrible punishment, hour after hour, as the Chinese wave broke over them. Major Pat Angier's body was brought back. His batman was in tears. The bodies of Lieutenants Curtis and Maycock could not be retrieved. The ambulances began to evacuate the wounded. Now "D" Company withdrew on Head-quarters, their young subalterns cocky, the men cheerful and resolute after a gruelling night's fighting at close range. Although Colonel Carne looked tired, his face grave, there was about him an unruffled calmness that gave great reassurance. Fresh dispositions were allotted to "A" and "D" Companies. A little after mid-day the last ambulance pulled out. We prepared for the battle we knew would inevitably develop that night. There was a spirit of confidence in our ability to hold on.

At about three o'clock that Monday afternoon the last hurried message from Battalion Rear Headquarters came over the air. It informed us that Chinese troops, some five miles behind us, were attacking in greatly superior strength, and that the situation was desperate. The battalion was cut off by a powerful and fast-moving enemy.

The road to safety was a tortuous one winding between steeply-rising mountain slopes: a paradise for guerrillas and enemy troops in ambush. Standing in the sunny hollow where main Headquarters lay I tried to realize the position. We were isolated by Chinese hordes intent on the kill. It was simply a matter of hours before darkness fell, and the lonely battalion would be assaulted on all sides in the nightmarish moonlight. Gloucester was 11,000 miles away. I longed to be able to say "Stop" to the rushing minutes: to prolong this quiet, sunny afternoon indefinitely.

A sinister hush seemed to lie in the towering mountains. Fear twisted inside me. The battalion doctor had carefully sewn up Major Angier's body in blankets. With the Adjutant, Tony Farrar-Hockley for congregation, I said the burial prayers. We bade farewell to Pat, laying his body out of the sun under an upturned assault-craft.

It grew to five o'clock and the troops queued for supper. In spite of the tense atmosphere everyone did his best to appear cheerful, but I found it impossible to enjoy the meal. The Adjutant moved about among the men, cracking jokes and dispersing many fears by his confident, bracing air and infectious smile. Night fell and the moon came up in its brilliance. Still all was quiet: the lull before the storm. At last the firing began in. the surrounding heights: battle was joined. The mortars at Headquarters began to bark, lobbing their missiles over the shielding hill into the advancing Chinese.

After midnight, "B" and "C" Companies were under overwhelming pressure, and Battalion Headquarters was menaced. The Colonel was compelled to order evacuation of the perimeter. There was not a moment to lose. Still the mortar-gunners kept up their fire at the hoarse, strident command of their sergeant-major. The first Chinese bullets sang across the bowl in which Headquarters lay. The order was given to withdraw, and concentrate upon the high ground on our left flank. "Support" company, and "Able" and "Dog" companies were already dug-in along the highest ridge. The doctor loaded me with dressings, bandages and medical supplies, and we set off for the gully leading up to the ridge. My field Communion case had to be abandoned. The slope was alive with scrambling, panting men. It was a stiff climb, and the tracer bullets began to whip across, their red witch-balls floating eerily. At last we reached comparatively safe ground, a sheltered plateau high above the valley. Dawn broke.

"B" Company, isolated and battered by innumerable Chinese waves, now began to withdraw from their hill with as much cover from our machine-guns and artillery as possible. It was a run for it: a drama acted out far below us. At last Major Harding and twenty men reached the gully leading to our ground, and wearily rejoined the Battalion.

Throughout Tuesday we lay disposed on this high ground. Our snipers, under Henry Cabral's direction, were active with harassing fire whenever the Chinese showed themselves in the valley below. It was a fairly quiet day, blue and warm. The wounded were attended to and I conducted one burial. It was very difficult to dig even a shallow grave in the hard, rocky earth. During the morning, a smouldering fire among the brushwood began to spread ominously, fanned by the breeze. Here was yet another difficulty. A party was detailed to beat it out.

We lacked food, water, batteries and ammunition. Courageous men went down the gully with the R.S.M., and under cover from machine-guns and smoke, raided our old dug-outs and trucks still standing at the foot of the ridge. They barely had time to get the goods and a small supply of biscuits and bully-beef. There was now enough replenishment to ensure the encircled Battalion small-arms defence for a limited time.

Everyone was outwardly calm and still hopeful. The spirit of the affair is epitomized by the Adjutant's instructions to a subaltern of "C" Company:

"Guy, you will stay here with your chaps unless you get orders from me to the contrary. If your ammunition runs out, hurl bloody rocks at them."

The signallers crouched over their gradually fading radios. Colonel Carne sat with his earphones on, in a small hollow, stolidly smoking the famous pipe. We knew that a strong relief column was attempting to get to us through the narrow defile. At first it was thought we might be relieved by mid-day. Noon came, and the men grew resigned. There was a report of a tank brewing-up, and blocking the advance of the rest. Everything seemed against us. It proved impossible for helicopters to land for our seriously wounded. The sense of our isolation became acute.

In the midst of all this, the spirit of the men of Gloucester Hill remained steady. A member of Support Company, being told by the Colonel that the whole battalion would very soon be brought up to the higher ridge for the last fight, said cheerfully, "We shall be all right, sir, 'twill be like the Rock of Gibraltar up here."

I sat and read some old letters, afterwards tearing them up with an awesome sense of finality. Towards sunset, 'planes flew low over the ridge and attempted an airdrop. It was disheartening to see the bundles missing our positions and falling inaccessibly on the lower slopes. Fortunately, plasma and blood transfusion equipment landed safely. Immediately the battalion doctor was able to set to work, and save a dying man's life there on the ridge.

As twilight came, we withdrew from our positions and climbed in single file to the topmost ridge of "Gloucester Hill" for the last desperate stand. It was a red sunset. The ridge commanded a superb view of the surrounding country and adjacent heights. In the darkness a thousand conflagrations, caused by napalm and shelling, glowed like camp-fires on the mountain slopes. We started to dig-in as best we could with the very few tools available. Everyone worked urgently with a driving sense of fear and necessity. I was only able to scrape a shallow trench in the stubborn ground. I walked about talking to men, trying to appear relaxed and hopeful, and feeling for encouraging words. It was far from easy. The medical aid post was sited in a hollow just below the line of the ridge. For most of the night this was my location.

A bugle shrilled in the darkness. Its haunting notes re-echoed and died away. Suddenly a light machine-gun started up its crackling chatter. Other weapons opened fire. The resonant stammering of the heavy machine-guns gave depth to the chorus. Shells from the British artillery, miles behind us, screamed weirdly over the ridge and crashed amidst the enemy on the slopes.

Along the ridge lay Battalion Headquarters, "Support" Company, and in a small hollow the medical aid post. To the north lay "Able" and "Dog", to the south combined "Baker-Charlie" Company and the mortar-gunners. The Chinese attacked from the south-east and up the approach from the north. The whole ridge of "Gloucester Hill" was swept by enemy fire. Machine-guns were firing on fixed lines from a hill to our west, and the medical post and "Support" Company's forward positions were threatened. At times, as the doctor and I lay in our shallow scrape, we could hear the bullets cutting the foliage some four feet above our heads. Mentally I prayed with a kind of fierce desperation. A more comforting sound was the rush and scream of our own shells, dropping to burst amidst the swarming enemy. We were within a curtain of steel.

From time to time, I heard the Adjutant's voice in different places in the darkness, shouting words of exhortation or advice to the hard-pressed troops. During the early hours, "A" Company, which had already suffered so heavily, was exposed to a Chinese storming assault and fell back dangerously. Suddenly there rang out brazenly the long reveille blown by Drum-Major Buss. There was a cheer from the hill's defenders. With amazing impudence "Drummie" followed this with "Come to the cookhouse door boys", and then the whole run of Army calls.

At dawn, "Able" counter-attacked, under the Adjutant's leadership, with magnificent courage and retook much lost ground. Repeatedly assaulted, they were not dislodged and continued to cover the northerly approach to the vital ridge. "D" Company was also taking heavy attack with a grim bravery. The southernmost defenders of the ridge were frequently disposed on forward slopes and from dawn were raked by heavy machine-gun and mortar fire. This they returned with great effect, but ammunition was running low and casualties mounted steadily. Our signals officer, Richard Reeve-Tucker, was killed instantaneously at this time. With almost irritating nonchalance, the Colonel moved to and fro in view of his men, amidst the hail.

In the cold morning light we awaited relief by a regimental combat-team of the 3rd U.S. Infantry Division. There was no food, and virtually no water. Wireless batteries were almost done. An impenetrable mist heaved below us like a sea of milk, blotting out all sight of the valley. As I crouched amidst a group of wounded I went back in memory to a ski-ing holiday at Chamonix. I remembered swinging up to the mountain top at Les Houches in the cable-cabin, and looking out over just such a rolling, milky mist as we saw now. An American 'plane swooped above us, so close we could see the pilot at the controls. He turned and ran in again. I waved my white handkerchief. Oh desperation, so close and yet so far! Mr. Hobbs called out, "They're coming up on all sides." A rich Gloucestershire voice shouted:

"Come on then, you bastards, and get your breakfast." Chinese bugles sounded—their slow, haunting notes hanging in the sharp air. American 'planes roared from the sky, strafing and rocketing with incredible precision all along the sides of the ridge. It was an inferno of tearing, screaming sound. Napalm scorched and seared the toiling enemy, but still he came on in inexhaustible numbers.

I was called to Sergeant Eames, M.M., of "Charlie" Company, who lay dying on a forward slope amidst the burnt, blackened undergrowth. He was severely wounded, and death was in his eyes. I prayed with him as he requested, and comforted him as best I could. The doctor ran down to him for some minutes to check his condition, but was very quickly called to other cases. The R.A.M.C. sergeant came and administered morphia. He, too, was called away. I remained with Eames for some time longer. He had been a real friend, and I was loath to leave him. Fighting for breath, he commissioned me most earnestly to write to his mother and his young wife. Then he said, "Leave me, padre, leave me. Get back, think of your safety, leave me." The filmy eyes closed, the words ceased. I scrambled back to the medical aid post. No stretchers were available. There was the possibility of a blanket-carry if a blanket could be found. I was conscious of a great mental weariness: logical thought became difficult. On the enemy hill slope opposite I could see many little figures moving about among the bare trees.

On my return to the aid post, I found the word had been passed that the battalion would withdraw. No outside relief was possible. The guns, miles behind us, were themselves now under Chinese small-arms fire and compelled to fight their way out. They could no longer provide us with artillery support. Throughout the long engagement the Commanding Officer's coolness, determination and moral strength had sustained us all with a sense of confidence, and a spirit of resistance. The men had fought with a calm, stubborn bravery, not for a moment contemplating defeat. The battalion had done all that could possibly be done: it was now no longer able to function effectively as a fighting unit. The order to withdraw was given: each company was to attempt a break-out of the Chinese encirclement as best it could. Sixteen miles of mountainous, enemy-infested country lay before the semi-exhausted troops. They began to pour off the fatal ridge in desperate but often jesting groups, disappearing into the deep, overgrown gullies. I urged especially the married men of the medical staff, along with my batman and driver, to make a run for it. I turned to the R.A.M.C. sergeant.

"This looks like a holiday in Peking for some of us," I said, smiling wanly. In a moment they were gone.

Sergeant Brisland of the Gloucesters remained with me.

At this time the medical officer, Captain Bob Hickey, was forward at Battalion Headquarters, where he had been doing magnificent work for the wounded. He rejected any thought of flight, and remained till the end carrying on his great ministry. Bob and I had no contact at this critical moment, but independently of each other we immediately decided to remain behind on the ridge. It was a spontaneous decision, without heroics, clearly indicated by duty. Only when Colonel Carne was satisfied that his stricken men, whom it was impossible to evacuate, had someone to care for them did he leave the ridge in a gallant attempt to lead a fighting patrol back to the U.N. lines.

As I knelt there in the aid post by the side of a grey-faced wounded man, I saw Major "Sam" Weller go down with his troops. He looked at me and shouted something. "Sam," I called out, "tell the Adjutant I'm staying with the wounded." A few moments later Major Guy Ward scrambled down. Sergeant Brisland was preparing to wave a white Red Cross flag for the protection of the aid post when Drum-Major Buss suddenly appeared on his own, moustache bristling, in the now deserted weapon-pit above us. He clutched his rifle, shouting at Brisland: "Put that white flag down, you . . ." It was clear that "Drummie" had not fully appreciated the situation. "The battalion's gone, drum-major. For heaven's sake run for it, man—it's your only chance," I yelled. He looked at me with amazement, and then was gone down the slope.

Some yards above me, to the left of the weapon-pit, a nineteen-year-old Gloucestershire lad lay dead, the vivid blood of youth welling from his mouth. I crawled up to him, and removed his rosary beads and letters. The letters I swiftly tore up, the beads I stuffed in my pocket. They were to remain with me throughout two and a half years of captivity. On my return to England I was able to give them to his parents.

A strange lull settled on the ridge. Some four or five able-bodied men stumbled into the aid post. I felt dazed, but not afraid. This seemed strange to me, because during the long battle I had known moments of acute fear. A mood of comparative nonchalance came over me. I looked along the ridge to the deserted ground held so gallantly by "A" Company. A solitary grenade burst there. At any moment I expected to see Chinese troops surge over the crest. They did not do so. A sudden terror seized me lest British guns should start shelling the ridge. "If that happens, we've had it," I thought. But even this consideration failed to grip my tired mind with any permanence. I spoke to a man on a stretcher at my side. He, too, seemed calm and resigned.

CHAPTER TWO

In Chinese Hands

SUDDENLY the first Chinese troops appeared above us, on the lip of the hollow in which the aid post lay: small, brown, extremely young-looking men. They were shabby and tattered, armed with new automatic weapons, and chattering excitedly. We raised our arms. Covering us with their weapons and shouting incomprehensibly, they motioned us to form in file. Bob Hickey, and the small group of prisoners with him, now joined us. We tried to demonstrate that we wished to carry our stretcher-cases with us, but the Communist soldiers would brook no delay. We were marched down the mountainside, our palms on our heads. After a short distance we were allowed to help our walking wounded as best we could.

Through a South Korean interpreter, also taken prisoner, the doctor and I asked the Chinese officer at the foot of the hill whether we could return, under guard, and carry our stretcher-wounded down into the valley. His reply was, "No. Do not fear. We, the Chinese People's Volunteers, will bring your wounded down later." This promise was, I believe, carried out—so far as I can judge. Later that afternoon, the Chinese deprived Bob of his remaining instruments and medical kit.

The Chinese guards threw us a tin of bully-beef and three loaves of bread (from our captured supply trucks), and brought water from a stream. This did not go far among some thirty-five of us, but it was our first food and drink, apart from a few biscuits, in nearly forty-eight hours. All afternoon we lay, exhausted physically and mentally, in a tree-covered gully looking across the small plain to the ground overlooking the Imjin. At about half-past three, we saw the remnants of the battalion being led in under Chinese guards. The gallant bids at a break-through had, for the most part, failed. The two and a half weary years of captivity by the Chinese Communists had begun.

That night, more than three hundred of us crossed the shallows of the Imjin River, carrying wounded on stretchers. It was a nightmare crossing. We stripped, except for our shirts rolled up to the armpits. We kept our boots on because of the sharp stones and barbed wire under water. A torrent of Chinese troops, baggage-carriers, mules and gun-carriages was pouring across in a tremendous uproar of confused sound. We made slow progress, holding our clothes in precarious bundles on our heads or handling the stretchers, fearing at every moment lest we should be trodden down in the darkness, or swept away into the deeps of the fast-flowing river.

As we entered the chilly water, the Adjutant of the Gloucesters bade me take his place at the front pole of the leading stretcher. "I'm going, padre." He was away in the darkness like a fish, borne rapidly downstream. As we stumbled painfully on, I prayed for his good success. If he could escape to our lines, there was so much comforting information about our survival he could give. Reaching the other bank, we hastily dressed, shivering with cold, the guards shouting excitedly and prodding us with their rifle-butts.

In the crossing, I had lost my underpants and a spare pair of thick socks, which I was bitterly to regret. We marched in heavy, sodden boots until near dawn, our throats and lips sore with thirst, our limbs fatigued to breaking point. The stretchers were a terrible liability. Some men gallantly did far more than their share of carrying, some took advantage of the darkness to evade the duty. At last we halted, falling asleep among bundles of straw in a Korean courtyard. Early in the morning, we received some lumpy, sweetened rice to eat, and that was all till next day.

That evening, after the Chinese had sifted our few personal possessions in search of knives, scissors, mirrors and the like, we marched on until midnight. To my chagrin, I dropped and lost my toothbrush, which, oddly enough, had remained with me through the battle. I was not to enjoy toothbrush or paste for the next six months. Another loss was my clerical stock and collar. I was greatly surprised when my batman restored it to me a couple of days later. He had been marching in another column, and had spotted a Korean peasant with it and retrieved it. This, I felt, was a remarkable example of service.

At midnight, we were lined up, and a high-ranking Chinese officer suavely addressed us in somewhat stilted English:

"Officers and soldiers of the British Army, you are now prisoners of the Chinese People's Volunteer Forces in Korea. You have been duped by the American imperialists. You are tools of the reactionary warmongers, fighting against the righteous cause of the Korean people, supported by their brothers the Chinese people. You are hirelings of the barbarous Rhee puppet-govern-

ment, but you will be given the chance to learn the
truth through study, and correct your mistakes. Do
not be afraid—we shall not harm you. At home, your
loved ones await you. Obey our rules and regulations,
and then you will not be shot."

That speech sounded the keynote of the celebrated
Chinese "Lenient Policy" towards war-prisoners. We
were "dupes", "tools", even "war-criminals" and "enemies of the people", but the "Lenient Policy" was to
preserve our lives, so that we could learn the truth. Later,
we were often addressed as "fellow-students"—that is,
of Marxism-Leninism.

We crowded into the stables and sheds allotted for the
night. Huddled together in cramping positions, we
attempted to sleep. At about two in the morning, I was
summoned for interrogation. An interpreter and a guard
led me away alone through the darkness. I entered a
small dug-out, some feet below ground. The military
interrogator, an impassive, quiet man, sat cross-legged at
a tiny table. One candle flickered in front of him. Behind
me in the shadows crouched several very youthful-looking
Chinese, two of whom spoke rather inadequate English.
They asked me to tell them as much as I knew about the
British 29th Brigade.

I produced my little Geneva Convention ticket, and
explained carefully that I could only give my name and
number. The Geneva Convention proved a red herring
of some consequence, and much excited Chinese discussion ensued. The upshot was, "We do not know about
Geneva Convention. You must obey his orders"—referring to the interrogator.

The interrogator handed me a long card, bearing the
names of various Army ranks from General downwards,

in English and equivalent Chinese script. I was to put my finger on my rank and function. I saw "Captain", but nowhere "Chaplain". Various functions were printed—"transport officer"; "engineers"; "artillery", but nothing remotely resembling the priestly office.

Here was a quandary. Devoutly raising my eyes to heaven, I made a large sign of the Cross upon myself, and folded my hands as in prayer, saying several times: "I am chaplain, priest, religious man—Christian teacher." The idea did not seem to sink in, and the interrogator began to speak more sharply in Chinese. The young interpreters set to work:

"You are captain."

"Yes—but I am a Christian priest, religious leader in the Army."

"You are captain. You are with your Commander Carne (as they pronounced it, 'Carnee'). What is your job?"

"I am . . .," and so it went wearily on.

Then, "Why you come Korea?"

"Because United Nations believe that North Korea invaded South Korea. This is unjust aggression. Therefore, our troops came to help South Korea. I am a chaplain, that is I . . .," and so on.

"But do you know that on July 25, 1950, South Korea invaded North Korea, supported by Wall Street warmongers and Anglo-American imperialist bloc? Why you come help this unjust war against Korean people?"

An hour must have gone by, and I felt dizzy.

"How many outfits in British brigade? How about artillery?"

"I do not know. I am religious leader, priest; I do not know any military information. I do not carry any gun."

More excited Chinese, then:

"You lie. You deceive Chinese Volunteers. We can punish unrighteous man."

The atmosphere was becoming rather angry. And then (such is Chinese unpredictability, about which we were to learn much), the military interrogator regained his impassivity, and contemptuously dismissed me with a wave of his hand. I was led away to the stable.

The next day passed monotonously and hungrily. We sat, for most of it, on a hillside, until the drizzle turned to drenching rain.

That night, I was again called for interrogation. There was a new interpreter. The chaplain idea must have got home, because:

"How many chaplains in British brigade?"

"I am not sure. I am only with Gloucesters." (Many of our captured men still had "Gloucester" on their shoulder-titles.)

"You meet other chaplains?"

"No. I am only with Gloucesters." (Bit of a white-lie here.) More discussion in Chinese, then:

"Where is chaplain with Ulster Rifles?"

"I do not know him."

The fencing match went on for about half an hour. I pleaded my ignorance of military and organizational matters. The interrogator began to drink steaming tea from a bucket brought in by an orderly. I longed for some, but no invitation was issued. However, when the officer put his cup down, I took it after two or three minutes and, dipping into the bucket, had a most welcome drink. This produced no hostile reaction and I gently repeated the performance.

I wrote down for them my name, number, rank and function. Tempers were in danger of rising again, and, seeking evasive action, I complied with a request for location of Gloucester by drawing a rough pencil sketch of England, showing the Bristol Channel and the approximate position of the city of Gloucester. I could not think that this would adversely affect the fortunes of the United Nations in Korea. I was again dismissed to my sleeping quarters. The following evening we continued our northward march. I was not with Colonel Carne's group, and did not see him again till six months later.

CHAPTER THREE

Six Strange Months

The Chinese Commander, Tien-Han, had large protruding ears and tiny, perfect, milky teeth. He always wore a cotton or silk choker high up round his neck, and appeared to be something of a dandy. He was said to be twenty-three years old.

His interpreter was a plumper, swarthy man with a burnt, bandaged face. We called him "Napalm-ni". He had extremely slant eyes. About his shoulders he wore a strip of crudely patterned carpet. He was altogether a man of piratical appearance. I was later told he was a university professor, and a "landlord's son", who had espoused the cause of "the people".

Before we set off, "Napalm" addressed us in his blurred English. After his instructions, he shouted "Do you know?" We yelled back "Yes".

The long, exhausting marches to the so-called "safe-rear" were mostly undertaken by night, for fear of accidental strafing by U.N. 'planes. We marched in a long, winding column, single-file, carrying our few personal belongings and heavy sacks of sorghum, our staple diet. During the hot days, we lay on tree-shaded hillsides, or crowded in Korean shacks, incessantly pestered by swarms of particularly noxious flies. Drinking water was not readily available. At about seven in the morning we received some hot, watery sorghum, and at six in the evening we ate either rice or sorghum. Very few of us had retained our mess-kit. Men were eating out of cigarette tins, and from cans picked up during the march and cleansed as well as possible. Some ate from their hats.

As darkness fell, we assembled in line of march, usually setting off about seven and reaching our destination any time between two and four-thirty the next morning. I recall vividly the terrible physical and mental weariness of the marches. Hour after hour, convoys of Chinese trucks passed, filling the air with the sickening smell of gasoline, and choking us with great clouds of dust from the primitive roads. Often, the headlights picked out for a moment the line of dust-enveloped prisoners as they filed round a bend.

It seemed like a vision from a Dantesque inferno—the bowed, sorrowful figures of the marching men seen for a moment in a reddish glow, the steep black sides of the cliff above, and far above all, the immense stretch of night-sky ablaze with millions of stars.

Sometimes 'planes zoomed above us, dropping flares which illuminated the road and adjacent hills. With desperate haste, we scattered like black beetles into the roadside ditches, lying face downwards with beating hearts, while the bombers hummed with agonizing persistence during endless minutes. All along the hilltops bordering the road, the Chinese "air-raid wardens", posted mile after mile, would shoot off their rifles at the sound of approaching aircraft. In obedience to the warning, trucks immediately switched off their lights, and came to a dead stop.

My own feeling, as I lay in the ditch on these occasions, was largely one of immense relief for a possible fifteen-minute rest from the gruelling march. Starting-up again at the command of our captors was agony. Overtaxed muscles had tightened, and the soles of our feet were indescribably tender. Somehow, we staggered on, until the rhythm of the march gripped us relentlessly once more. Every so often, the Chinese halted us for about twenty minutes. This was sheer bliss, to be followed by the pain of recommencing the march, which always seemed eternal—across plains, through valleys, across rivers, up mountains. We dreaded long bridges. In fear of marauding aircraft, the Chinese would goad us into a stumbling run, lasting several hundred yards, to get us quickly clear of these dangerous targets.

At last, we would halt in a village and crouch, too tired to think, our bodies quickly cooling at the sharp chill of the early morning. The Chinese commander would deliver an incomprehensible tirade to his men, his assistants meanwhile going to and fro with flashlights, trying to arrange accommodation for us. As I look back on these fantastic nights, I seem to feel again the appalling tiredness and to hear the strange, unceasing roar of the bullfrogs from the surrounding paddy-fields, and the high-pitched voice of the Commander scolding somewhere in the darkness.

Early on the first Sunday morning of captivity, we were lying on a hillside, chilled, filthy and hungry. Depression lay like a black cloud. In my pocket I had a little copy of the famous seventeenth-century spiritual classic, *The Practice of the Presence of God*, by Brother Lawrence. Seeking comfort, I opened it and read the familiar words on the first page. Someone records his opening conversation with Brother Lawrence, and how Lawrence tells him that: "In the winter, seeing a tree stripped of its leaves, and considering that within a little time the leaves would be renewed, and after that the flowers and fruit appear, he received a high view of the Providence and Power of God, which has never since been effaced from his soul."

I looked up, and saw above me a bare branch with the white blossoms at its tips already bursting in the sun, outlined against a blue sky. The coincidence struck me forcibly. It seemed like a message. I felt a sudden rush of hope and absurd joy. I jotted down the date on the dogeared flyleaf: Sunday, April 29, 1951. Nearby, the youthful Chinese guard stared at me sullenly, cleared his throat raucously and spat on the tree-trunk, watching the spittle run down like a thread of silver.

After nine nights of marching, we arrived at "half-way house" on the Taedong River, some forty-five miles above Pyongyang. Here, we rested for forty-eight hours, and Chinese cameramen took a group photograph. I was summoned for interrogation. The atmosphere was outwardly quite friendly:

"You believe in God?"

"Yes."

"Is it an idea of God to send bad things?"

"God does not send bad things, but often, owing to the badness of men, bad things happen."

"Why does your God allow Korean people to suffer at the hands of the Anglo-American brigands?"

Familiar ground, but the opportunity was too limited for an essay in theodicy, nor would my interrogators' English have proved adequate. I sat under the trees amidst a group containing the man with the burnt face we called "Napalm-ni"; a podgy, black-plaited woman known to us as "the Fat Girl"; and a smooth young man whose name was J. C. Kahn. After some verbal sparring I was asked:

"Who is the unjust aggressor in Korea?"

"I believe in the United Nations, and the United Nations have said that North Korea is the aggressor."

"You must learn something. You do not understand the problem. You must study hard with our comrades."

That night, the column marched on, minus some thirty-six prisoners who were weak from dysentery. At the last moment, I and four other officers were called out, and marched away in the darkness to a tiny Korean village about three miles off. This was to be my home for the next four months. We slept in a filthy shack along with some fifteen prisoners who were sick. Daily washing facilities did not exist. Flies were legion. Men tore strips of dirty Korean newspaper from the walls to roll a few, pitiful shreds of tobacco. The guard would report to the leader, and a lecture against "destroying the people's property" ensued.

Days of utter boredom and monotony followed. At five in the morning, unless it rained, we were roused from our crowded sleeping quarter, and marched to the cover of the trees on a hillside. Here we remained all day till six in the evening, talking among ourselves; thinking; sleeping; watching the Korean peasants at their spring sowing in the valley. All day the cuckoo called, rending our hearts with home-sickness. Flights of 'planes passed over regularly, often ringed by shell-bursts from the Communist batteries some miles away. At morning and evening we had sorghum (sometimes rice) and bean shoots; at mid-day boiled water.

The theme of my prayer at this time was: "O my God, I praise and bless thy wondrous Name for all thy mercy and thy love." A slow, meditative saying of the Te Deum was wonderfully rewarding, and a corrective for depression.

From time to time, I held short, informal services and spoke of God, giving what comfort I could. But the officers and myself were separated from the men on the hillside, and to be seen mingling with the other ranks, and especially talking to them, usually brought interference from the guards. Officers and men were frequently interrogated. The Chinese left me alone, but men told me that the interrogators often asked about me—my name, my job, rank, what I spoke about, and whether I was liked by the troops.

The sick got a little better and moved northwards to the prison-compounds. Some of them died later.

Other prisoners came to the village, but went north after a short interval. It was a great disappointment to see the Adjutant of the Gloucesters brought in after his gallant attempts at escape to our lines. He had badly-poisoned feet. By late July (1951), there were only eight of us left in the village, and we remained there under Chinese guard until the latter part of August. These eight were Guy and Carl (both artillery officers); Tony; Byrom and Duncan, both U.S.A.F.; Thomas Batilo of the Philippines; Sergeant Fitzgerald and myself.

It was interesting to observe the Chinese soldiers' routine. Early in the morning they did weapon-drill. After breakfast they attended lengthy indoctrination sessions given by the political commissar. You would have known him immediately as R.A.E.C. (Chinese equivalent). These sessions were always prefaced by vigorous singing. A blackboard, maps and diagrams were often used. In the hot noon they slept. Later they would often hold what appeared to be "self-criticism" periods, or play games. Air-raid precautions were most scrupulously observed. At the cry of "Fiji-lay-lah", all went to earth under the thick foliage.

We lived squalidly, unwashed for long periods, unshaven, foul-smelling, our bodies a breeding-ground for lice. I told my comrades that I looked forward to the day when I should stand in the pulpit of a fashionable West End church and say: "My dear brethren, have you ever been lousy?" Every morning we spent a ritual two hours turning our clothes inside out and killing about fifty lice each. I had a pocket New Testament, from which I often read to my comrades. I said prayers, in which the group gladly joined. In two cases I laid hands on the chronically sick and blessed them. We felt strongly that we were in the hand of God.

Daily indoctrination began by a young and obviously intelligent, though fanatical, Chinese student-Marxist, who spoke pretty good English. This was J. C. Kahn. In a surprisingly ingratiating atmosphere, we were given lectures on such topics as:

> "Corruption of the U.N. by the American war-mongers."
> "The Chinese people's right to Formosa."
> "The Stockholm Peace Appeal."
> "Progress in People's China."
> "Churchill, tool of the Truman-MacArthur-Dulles fascist clique."
> "The Soviet Union heads the World Peace Camp."

We were invited to put our point-of-view, but needless to say, we were always wrong. It was forever a case of: "You have an incorrect attitude. You must study hard and learn the truth." Our smooth-faced mentor, immaculate in well-pressed olive-greens, his glasses shining, would sometimes sit among his bearded tramp-like charges, delicately tearing a grasshopper limb from limb while he talked of "Wall Street's aggressive war in Korea". Guards with fixed bayonets stood on duty a few yards away. In the trees the cicadas twanged ceaselessly like an orchestra of jews-harps.

Often in the evenings, as twilight fell, the Chinese would dance and sway in weaving columns to the barbaric sound of a drum and clashing cymbals. This was the ancient "Yang-Ko" dance.

A new guard-company took over, and our daily living conditions improved. We were given the chance to wash daily (but without soap or towels); we were given some anti-malarial tablets and louse powder, and our food, twice each day, from the Chinese troops' kitchen, became quite palatable. An eleven-day tobacco issue commenced, with a small quantity of cigarette paper. This was really living. Our first dip in the Taedong River was a great event for us. As I strode in, with long, matted hair and beard, I heard a laughing voice shout: "Padre, you look just like John the Baptist in the River Jordan!"

We rose at first light and retired at twilight. Monotony and boredom ate into us. Sometimes, armed interpreters would take us for evening strolls or a dip in the river. Inevitably conversation drifted to John Foster Dulles, or the Chinese people's right to Taiwan. Once, we attended a Chinese tea-party, sitting cross-legged round big bowls of steaming tea and smoking "Dragon" cigarettes from Peking, while the Commander asked us through his interpreters what we thought of the Chinese, of the war in Korea, and the possibility of peace. They insisted on our singing something. After much embarrassment, I obliged with "In Dublin's fair city".

The other side to this odd existence was seen in the punishment of several officers who had refused to impart military information, or who had attempted escape. They were punished by confinement, arms bound, in dank underground holes, shut away from the sun and fresh air for considerable periods. By this time, the Chinese had realized my status as chaplain, and I was not summoned for interrogation for a long period. They concentrated on people who obviously "knew something". As for the Filipino officer, he was urged by them to sever his connections with us for, they said, "You are an Asian man, you should be on our side."

At last, in the latter part of August, we moved. To our surprise, we went south, passing on foot through shattered Pyongyang. We crossed the Taedong by the huge girder-bridge, which was thronged with traffic. We marched for ten days, sometimes in terrific heat; sometimes in torrential downpours; staying in Korean villages; sometimes lying in ditches while U.N. 'planes rocketed overhead strafing the road we had just run from, filling the air with one vast, splitting roar. We were unscathed, except that one of our number received a cheek abrasion from a flying cartridge case. Every village seemed packed with Chinese.

At about two o'clock in the morning, during a particularly long-drawn-out march, I collapsed and was unable to go on. The fast-moving column was soon out of sight. An interpreter and a guard remained with me. I recovered after fifteen minutes, and we went on. I was utterly exhausted, and fell a second time. Kicks, abuse and pistol-cocking failed to move me—I was past caring.

Then occurred an act of simple, human kindness I can never forget. Some Chinese infantry passed in the moonlight, and several soldiers stopped. I was vaguely aware of new voices, then of supporting arms and of garlic breath in my face. Cold, wonderfully cold water, was put to my lips and splashed on my forehead. A heap of sugar was placed in my palm, and then a few small biscuits. There was friendly laughter. I was helped to my feet, my pack was taken by someone, and I was assisted along the road for several miles I suppose, my arm round the neck of a sturdy peasant-soldier, who kept saying encouragingly, "Sleefo soon, sleefo". At last, in a confused roar of noise, I was aware of being lifted, and then of a current of air passing swiftly and exquisitely over me. I was on a lorry. Towards dawn I was taken to a tiny room where my comrades were lying in the sleep of exhaustion.

Because of our swollen, bleeding feet, Fitzgerald and I were allowed to march by day at our own pace. Daily we set off with our guards at six, and marched like weary old men until nine at night, halting for two blessed hours at mid-day.

At the end of August, we arrived at our new village. Soon we were visited by an important political personage we had met before. This was "Hawk-face". He was accompanied by "the Fat Girl", and a nebulous, smiling character from the last village called Commander Lee, who was said to have "something to do with all war-prisoners". He was tall, thin and rather good-looking. We asked why we had been marched south, and why we were not sent to a proper P.O.W. camp. The reply was: "You must study hard and learn the truth. Soon you will go to a camp in the safe rear. The prisoners are very happy there. They are studying hard and learning the truth." It all sounded terribly familiar.

That night, two of our company, Tony and Duncan, escaped while we were asleep, and I did not see them again till January, 1952, when they were admitted to P.O.W. Camp 2 up on the Yalu. The next morning a hue-and-cry broke out. I was summoned for interrogation:

"Why did you not tell us they were going to escape?"

"I did not know."

"You did not know? You are a priest—they tell you everything."

"They did not tell me."

"What have they taken with them? Which way have they gone?"

"I do not know."

"You lie."

"No, I do not lie. I am a Christian priest."

"Yes, you do not lie to the Protesterians, but to us, the Chinese People's Volunteers, you lie. You are a cunning priest."

An angry conversation followed between the Commander and the interpreter.

"You are a liar. You have a hostile attitude to us. You must be punished. Every day they are away, you will get punishment."

My heart sank. This probably meant days in "the hole" under ground, trussed up like a chicken. I was sent back to the other five. The day wore on and night came. At last the dread summons came for me. I stood before the interpreter:

"What is your full name, age and date of capture?"

A form was filled. Then, "Take this tobacco for your

friends. Tell them we are trying to get more. Go back."
Chinese unpredictability again.

We were allowed to write one short letter. Our address
was quoted to us as c/o "The Chinese People's Volunteers'
P.O.W. Corps." My letter did not reach home.

One night, while we slept, a Chinese guard (or possibly
a North Korean peasant) rifled my pack. Among the
things he took was my little India-paper New Testament
(presumably to roll cigarettes). It was a tragic loss, not
only for me, but for the others, as it was our only Bible.
The thought of facing perhaps two or three more years
without a Bible was extremely depressing. I prayed
earnestly that somehow or other I might obtain a
Testament. This prayer was to be richly answered a little
later in the year.

At this time, our condition was somewhat dismal. Of
the six of us left, two were dangerously weak and thin
from prolonged dysentery. Our food was very poor—
millet and ground-nuts without variety. We slept huddled
together in a draughty shack, recently used for stabling
ponies. Night temperatures were getting very low as
October approached. The Chinese seemed very bored,
and our daily dose of Marxism had ceased. At our
request, a Chinese doctor came and was helpful to our
sick men. We rose on the guards' command at first light,
and were allowed to swill our faces with water from the
well. Then, shivering with cold, we were marched to the
shelter of a hedge bordering a bean-field. There we passed
the day, longing first for breakfast, then for the warmth
of the late September sun. At this time I was suffering
from scalp irritation, caused by infestation by head-lice.

To our intense surprise, a Chinese officer came one day
and produced our watches, fountain-pens and rings that

had been taken from us five months previously, which we had not thought to see again. We discussed this lengthily amongst ourselves: perhaps the war had ended, perhaps we were going home, perhaps, perhaps . . .

The next day, Michaelmas Day, we were marched off to join a group of captured G.I.s and South Koreans. Our two sick men were left behind. We did an arduous three-day march over the mountains to a mining village, which bore all the signs of having accommodated prisoners before.

CHAPTER FOUR

North to the Yalu

It was October 1, a big revolutionary feast day for the Chinese Communists, when we arrived at the mining camp (so called because of its proximity to a Korean mining community). The recently-captured G.I.s and South Koreans were with us. We were soon separated. After officials had checked our identity and thoroughly searched us, taking away my few religious booklets and meagre belongings, we were marched to a dirty, tumbledown shack which was far too well-ventilated for the time of year.

Here, Randle, a young captive officer of the 8th Hussars, who had miraculously survived a late parachute drop from a burning 'plane, joined our tiny British group. Since capture he had been confined with American white and negro troops, and a few Puerto Ricans. I was overjoyed to hear that he had organized regular Bible-reading and prayers. He had been given pork and chicken by his captors in honour of October 1, and encouraged us to think we might receive the same. Our mouths drooled. We had been marching over the mountains, helping sick and weakened men, since 5 a.m. and had had only one rice meal. We were feeling exhausted and cold. It was now 4 p.m. It was therefore a great disappointment to receive, an hour later, our old friends sorghum and ground-nuts. We spent the night huddled together for warmth, having only a couple of rice-sacks for the group.

The next day the Chinese showed us their better side, moving us to a more reasonable room and giving us lathes, paper and paste to close up the gaping windows. In view of the increasing cold, they gave us a quilt for each pair and some more rice sacks. With these, and sleeping in our clothes, we kept reasonably warm at nights. Food improved, too, and we received during our eleven days' stay here some pork, steamed bread and daily rice with boiled water to drink. Each morning we rose at seven to do callisthenics, followed by a swill in the icy stream and breakfast at eight. The next meal was at four. Soviet magazines (in English), and Shanghai papers were issued. Each day we made a six-mile "wood-run" to collect sawn logs from the mountain sides. The days developed into blue, warm ones by about eleven, and we returned after handling our four-man loads looking forward to a rub-down in the river, even though soap, towels and toothbrushes were still lacking.

About the fourth day some fifty Americans arrived, all looking very tired, though their spirits were cocky. We learned that these men had been selected much earlier in the year for special indoctrination and treatment as "peace-fighters", or "peace champions". They had been promised an early return to the U.N. lines, their captors hoping they would be good pro-Communist, anti-U.N. propaganda. Some of them had made individual or group-statements, broadcast over Peking radio, or published in Communist newspapers. Now they were disillusioned, and becoming hopelessly reactionary as Chinese promises evaporated. They, too, were going north. They were blessed with unspeakable wealth, for they had soap, towels with red stars on them, and firm,

4

hygienic-looking tooth-brushes and paste. Next morning it felt really good to be soapy again after five long months! That night the erstwhile "peace-fighters" struck up a raucous "God Bless America" in the darkness, until the guards, on instructions from the interpreters, came in and put a stop to it.

Towards the end of our stay, the Chinese returned to me my religious booklets. They confiscated my little copy of the "Geneva Convention regarding war-prisoners" because, as they said:

"This is not necessary. We know how to treat you. We go by International Law."

They also objected strongly to a newspaper cutting I happened to have in my wallet, in which the Bishop of Manchester was reported as saying that Communism was a religion.

"This is a lie and hypocrisy," said the chief interpreter. "Communism wants to set up a righteous society here in this world, but religion teaches you to hope for an ideal life after death. We do not believe in a life after death, therefore Communism is not a religion."

On October 11 we commenced a march north to the Yalu, which was to take sixteen days. The other four British officers were sick or wounded and could not march. They were put in a lorry, and did the journey within four or five nights. I was the sole remaining Britisher to do the long march. I had with me my faithful Filipino friend, Thomas—a fervent Catholic and a devoted companion, to whom I owe much. So we set off, a tousled gang of G.I.s, ex-"peace-fighters", and one British chaplain. The South Koreans marched separately, by now apparent converts to Communism. They had adopted the North Korean "Kim Il Sung" anthem, and sang "The East is Red" with a quite moving sincerity. They looked at us with increasing coldness and suspicion.

This march was by day, with frequent stops sprawled in ditches while the U.N. 'planes passed over on their daily missions. We saw the wild, natural grandeur of Korea at first-hand. Day after day we marched on a bellyful of rice from six in the morning till four in the afternoon, sinking, too tired to talk, on the wooden floors of school-houses, or on straw in barns and stables. Within an hour and a half the welcome rice and potato soup would appear. After that, oblivion.

Our Chinese leader was a certain Captain Ho, who had the pernickety habit of lining us up after the march, and saying sententiously, "Comrades, we have reached to-light's destilation." On one occasion "a comrade" called out:

"Stuff it, you sonofabitch."

Captain Ho was aghast. The guards were alerted.

"Come out the boy who said that." (Captain Ho was wont to call us "boys").

Silence.

"Stand out," he screamed.

No movement. Then followed a long lecture on bad language, the captain assuring us that "only rascals and tools of the reactionary imperialists use such words".

The march led us over mountain crests; up to our necks through rushing torrents—a living chain of prisoners and Chinese; through deep forests; along sandy, remote roads. The devastation of North Korean towns by aerial bombardment was complete. The people were living in dug-outs and hovels, and abject poverty and distress were visible everywhere. Nevertheless, one could not escape the impression of a calm, independent and resolute populace in the midst of horror. It was tragic to see the burnt-out shells of large churches and schools: an inevitable accompaniment of air-warfare. Sometimes we saw groups of Caucasian technicians passing by in lorries, or standing in groups outside Korean cottages, looking at us stonily.

At odd times, but especially on the two Sundays of the march, I held service for the prisoners. The Americans were most grateful, many of them having seen no chaplain since capture. A New Testament was loaned to me by one of the group, and I felt my prayer for replacement of my own stolen Bible was being answered in part. The prisoners crowded into the shack to hear the Scriptures read, to join in the prayers, to listen to a short sermon and to receive a blessing. On the first Sunday, after such a service, Captain Ho called for me:

"Why did you assemble the boys?"

"It is Sunday, our Christian Holy Day. We had prayers. I am a priest."

"What did you say to them?"

"I spoke about Jesus Christ."

"Did you say anything else?"

"I asked them to pray for their homes and for peace."

"Why did you not get my permission to assemble the boys?"

"I did not think it was necessary."

"You must ask me always. This time I only warn you. Go back."

The second Sunday, I asked Ho well before, and after the usual "I will consider it" he gave permission. As I was reading the Bible, the guard entered. Chattering with annoyance he came to my shoulder. In dead silence from the room, I continued reading. With a hiss, the guard suddenly tore the Bible from my hand and strode out with it, gazing at it upside down. He doubtless thought he was doing his duty, and obviously felt he had scotched some foul plot against the Chinese. I was very upset to think we had lost yet another precious Bible. But Ho again called for me, and returned the little Testament about two hours later.

At last, exhausted and wet to the skin after a long final march through driving snow, we arrived at a big prisoner-of-war camp. It was October 26. For a shivering half-hour we waited, until a group of Chinese officials came to inspect and address us. We entered a barn-like shed, open on two sides to the weather. We were lined up, and from the depths of chill misery heard the Camp Commander begin with: "Fellow-students, we welcome you to this camp . . ."

After that, we stripped naked and were given thin blue uniforms, absurd blue hats and good padded overcoats. Accommodation was arranged in unheated, clay-and-wattle hovels. I was placed in a G.I. compound. It was Chong-Song camp.

The compound contained many very sickly and dirt-grimed prisoners, often crawling with lice. There was filth everywhere, and the lean-to latrines were in an indescribable state. Owing to the physical weakness of many men, and Chinese obstructiveness towards their leaders, an atmosphere of heartbreak prevailed. The G.I.s told me that no religious gatherings were permitted. However, for the first time I experienced three meals a day—sorghum, steamed bread, beans and vegetables. Sheer luxury!

I was told that the British officers had left the vicinity a week ago. My heart leapt to learn of Gloucester sergeants nearby. An American lad asked me to come with him to the G.I. kitchen. On my arrival there, a cheerful youngster from New York greeted me:

"Guess you're the British chaplain. Yeah? Say, I've heard a lot about you, sir."

I was charmed.

"Say, chaplain, I wanna present you with this. This li'l ole good book belonged to my buddy. He got killed, sir. I sure would like for you to have it."

Tears welled in my eyes.

"Son, you don't know it, but you're an answer to my prayer."

Here I was with a New Testament again—all my own. It was a big thing. My comrade of the recent march had, of course, wanted his precious Bible back and he had gone to a different compound. Yes, I felt my prayers were yielding fruit. More was to come. A day later I sneaked into the British sergeants' compound. Here was a blessed reunion to melt the heart. I was given a good hot bath in a tub, with soap and spotless towel; my lousy underclothes were taken away and boiled; and a Gloucester sergeant presented me with a New Testament:

"A padre's not much good without one or two of these, and we've already got one. You have it, sir."

Here was the second wonderful answer to my prayer.

To mix again with these magnificent sergeants was a tonic that lifted my morale to the heavens. The next evening, as twilight came, I was summoned by the Chinese and put with several American officers on a lorry. "You will go to another camp." I was thrilled because I guessed this meant seeing Colonel Carne and the Gloucester officers again. The lorry drove away, and soon we were travelling by a tortuous route along the twisting line of the Yalu. As I sat looking into a crimson sunset from the back of the open lorry I felt a sense of peace and relaxation. I could not guess that two long years of captivity lay ahead. We drove on through the darkness, and after five hours arrived at Pyuktong, the infamous P.O.W. Camp 5.

Standing in the dark outside a group of buildings, while our interpreter got instructions about us, I suddenly heard a voice say in homely Scottish tones:

"Hello. This is Marine Andrew Condron speaking. Hello, Mum, Dad and all at home. By courtesy of the Chinese People's Volunteers I am broadcasting to you now, to tell you how we are getting on here, and about our preparations for Christmas . . ."

Andrew Condron's has since become a controversial name, for he is the only British soldier who wished to remain with the Communists at the time when the prisoners were exchanged.

I spent one night and morning at Pyuktong, billeted with the Turks. When they knew I was a chaplain, they showed me all possible kindness and helpfulness, treating me as one of the prophets, giving me precedence in everything and waiting upon me hand and foot.

I went before a camp official. He retained my paper-backed British "Army Prayer Book". I asked strongly for it, but:

"You cannot keep it."

"But why, it is a Christian prayer-book?"

"No, it is a military document. It says 'Army Prayer Book'. Prisoners cannot keep Army documents."

Later in the morning I joined a group of American officers, and we went over the mountain-pass on foot to Pi-chong-ni, some ten miles away. It was Prisoner-of-War Camp No. 2, and as we passed the sentries into the barb-wired compound, I felt I had reached "home". Most of the captured Gloucester officers and others were here, and many American officers, too. This was to be my "parish behind barbed wire" from now, October 31, 1951, until August 19, 1953.

Since my capture on April 25, 1951, I had marched more than 600 miles with the Chinese. I felt proud of this achievement. By a paradoxical turn of events, it had been left to me, the chaplain, to do more foot-slogging as a prisoner-of-war than any other captured member of the 29th Infantry Brigade.

I had learnt much since capture, but my experience of Chinese Marxists was only just beginning.

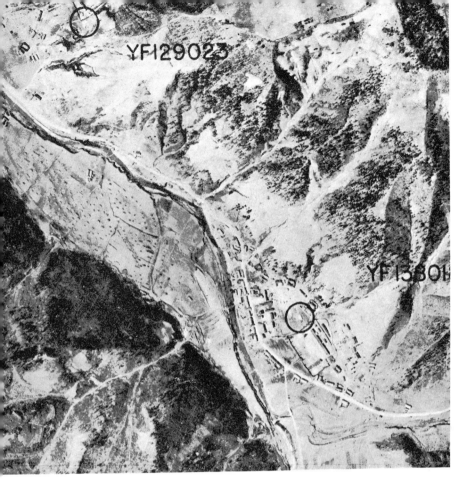

Aerial view of Prisoner-of-War Camp 2, Pi-chong-ni, North Korea, showing No. 1 Company Compound (YF 138018) and, as from October 16th, 1952, No. 2 Company Compound (YF 129023).

3. The whole camp of approximately 370 British and American prisoners was originally concentrated in the compound at YF 138018. From October 16th, 1952, the new compound held No. 2 Company. During the summer of 1952 we had hauled logs and carried clay for the building of this compound.

Circles are drawn round the large white boards placed just outside each compound. The marking in their centres can be seen. These boards identified the compounds from the air as prisoner-of-war camps. The perimeters are clearly delineated by the line of barbed-wire and fencing.

I lived in No. 1 Company compound, my "parish behind barbed-wire", in the squad-room at the extreme right wing of the long Korean schoolhouse. The square building immediately beyond, and within the wire, is the Company Commander's H.Q. Beyond that, outside the wire, is the Camp Medical H.Q. Behind the long school-house lie the barber's shop, the carpenter's shed, and Chinese officials' sleeping quarters. The camp-kitchen is bottom right. The long shadows of the poplars bordering the compound, my "Seven Sentinels", can clearly be seen, left-centre, just beyond the path leading up to the compound from the main village highway. The left wing of the long schoolhouse was the camp lecture-room, library and chapel (for two hours on Sundays).

The parade and recreation ground was the scene of roll-call, shake-down, soccer, volley-ball, and American base-ball.

Outside the wire, with the black circle running through it, lies Camp Commander Ding's ("Snake-eyes") H.Q. and residence. Here lived Madame Ding, and their plump little daughter, aged four.

The long narrow building beyond is where the Chinese staged their big "Germ Warfare" photographic exhibition. Beyond that again is Camp H.Q. I was from time to time interrogated here by Comrade Chen ("Scar-face") and Comrade Sun.

Moving left from the circle (YF 138018), can be seen the Chinese troops' H.Q. The big building well back from the road, second along from the extreme left angle of our compound, second row of build-ings from the road, is the warehouse. On the front edge of the square and bordering the road is the notorious "jail on the road". Immediately to the left of the big warehouse, and running trans-versely to it, are the jail cells where the Adjutant of the Gloucesters; Corporal Abbot, U.S.A.F.; C.S.M. Morton of the Gloucesters, and myself were imprisoned in solitary.

In the lone house on the left of the road, and immediately before the last house (extreme right of photograph) Colonel Carne was held for part of his solitary confinement.

Moving down the road towards the compound of No. 1 Company, the first large house with courtyard seen on the left of the road below Colonel Carne's house, was the Camp Hospital. I was forbidden to visit here, even under guard, from February 8th, 1952 onwards.

(United States Air Force photo).

4. Our Chalice, a Chinese soldier's tin mug. It was used for the five celebrations of Holy Communion the Chinese permitted us in two and a half years' captivity.

5. The wooden Communion Paten carved by Major Ryan, inscribed "Behold, the Bread of Angels".

4. This was the best we could do for a chalice : a green tin mug marked with a black cross. Major Ryan did his best to make a wooden one. He carved it beautifully, but unfortunately it would not hold liquid. Wood tended to split very quickly. We sealed it with wax, but without success. When water was poured in experimentally, it gradually seeped and a drip began. We dare not risk this with the wine to be sacramentally consecrated.

Our Chinese captors gave us wine and bread on five occasions for Holy Communion. They rejected my request for a monthly celebration, and refused our demand that their delegates at Panmunjom ask on our behalf for Communion vessels, prayer-books and chaplain's vestments.

5. For the first celebration of Holy Communion in P.O.W. Camp 2, at Christmas 1951, we used half of a British mess-tin for a paten. Before our second one, at Easter 1952, Major Ryan carved this simple wooden paten, using a knife made from a steel stay from an American officer's boot. A few days after this Easter, Major Ryan was taken out of the compound for interrogation. He went into solitary for intransigence, and I did not see him again until sixteen months later, at the Communist transit camp near the Panmunjom prisoner-exchange point.

CHAPTER FIVE

The Prisoners of Pi-Chong-Ni

In P.O.W. Camp No. 2, at Pi-chong-ni on the Korean-Manchurian border, I had a consoling reunion with Colonel Carne, and with most of the captured British officers from the 29th Brigade. On my return to England two years later, the time came when I saw, as though from an immense height, a neat bird's-eye view of my parish behind barbed wire, where I had spent such a strange, anxious time in the hands of the Chinese. I assured myself inwardly: "You are in England; you are free; all this is behind." It was a great moment.

P.O.W. Camp No. 2 was the officers' compound, some ten miles away from No. 5, the big other ranks' camp at Pyuktong. It was an area about 110 by 70 yards, enclosed by barbed wire and fencing, with sentry posts at intervals. Parallel with the village street, and within the wire, was a line of seven stately poplars. I used to call them "the Seven Sentinels". Beyond the wire the life of the Korean hamlet of Pi-chong-ni went on its traditional way. Superimposed on this pattern was the busy life of the Chinese garrison and prisoner-of-war Corps staff, who were billeted in the village. The camp lay in a natural bowl with steep mountains rising all round. Some three hundred and seventy British and American officers lived in a long Korean schoolhouse, divided by wooden partitions into small rooms, a squad of thirty men to a room. In the sub-zero winter each squad-room had a tiny wood-burning stove. It was difficult to keep warm, and many weary hours were spent crouched round them. Fifteen men slept along each wall. Except for a narrow aisle down the centre of each room, the floor-boards were covered by straw mats. On these mats we slept, literally shoulder to shoulder. There were no individual sleeping-bunks built until February, 1953; these served for the last six months.

There was also the camp-kitchen with its primitive ovens and big cooking pots, a lecture room, and the lean-to communal latrine, which afforded precious little shelter from the biting January winds. An unavoidable visit here at about two o'clock of a winter's morning, with the temperature at 35-40 degrees below zero, was a harrowing experience. On Sundays and other occasions the lecture-room was used by us for our religious gatherings. It was our only chapel.

Each squad had an American or British squad-leader appointed by our captors; a Chinese platoon leader, and an interpreter. In the compound lived the Chinese Company Commander, who changed about every four months. He was liable to deliver tedious Chinese speeches, often more in sorrow than in anger, which were translated to us in the most naïve and amusing English. I shall always remember these gems, and the wild hoots of laughter with which they were greeted.

"No man can be sick without getting the permish."

"At last we have got tomatoes for you: we know you
are crazy about them."

"When the Commander speaks, no man can joke and
make the strange noises."

And in reference to some new summer uniforms for
the prisoners:

"They are very fashionable, from Shanghai, with
brass buttons."

Above the Company Commander was the Camp
Commander, who lived with his wife and small daughter
in a well-guarded house at H.Q., beyond the barbed wire.
He was an immaculately-dressed, aristocratic-looking
man, with a pale, cold face and beautiful, slim hands.
This was Commander Ding, known to us all as "Snake-
eyes". He seemed to speak no English. Ding would
saunter through the compound from time to time with
a remote hauteur which was quite impressive. The time
was to be when we saw him come through our compound
in a very different manner, but that is later in the
story. . . .

"Snake-eyes" regularly delivered full-dress three-hour
orations in the lecture-room, in Chinese. These were
usually translated in well under half the time. A popular
theme was "The U.N. warmongers hold up the Panmunjom peace-talks", but his greatest effort was "The
Lenient Policy". His interpreter was a clever young
Chinese, who spoke remarkably good idiomatic English.
This was Wong (called by us "D.P." Wong, because of
his tirades against the American habit of carrying pin-up
girls in their wallets. These he remorselessly branded as
"dirty pictures"). Other officials rejoiced in the nick-

names of "Tilt"; "Smilin' Jack"; "Pig-face"; "Burly"; "Scar-face" and "The Hatchet-man".

From November, 1951, to April, 1952, we had four hours of lectures daily, and two to three hours of "group study and discussion". Very early in the morning, the loudspeaker blared Soviet and Chinese revolutionary music over our compound, beginning with "Arise ye prisoners of starvation; arise ye wretched of the earth." This seemed to us particularly appropriate. We were on the parade-ground at 7 a.m. for roll-call, followed by physical jerks. This was a bizarre scene in the frosty twilight of a January morning. For an hour before breakfast at 8.30, the squad-leader or "monitor" would have to read to the group from some Communist publication. At ten, the warning bell summoned us to the bare, icy lecture-room, where we sat Oriental-fashion on the floor-boards, toes and ears freezing, while the evil machinations of the U.N. were exposed, "American imperialism" flagellated, or the "happy life of the Soviet people" eulogized. At 12.30 we broke off: we dozed, paced the compound, drank hot water (sometimes hot bean-milk) and gossiped. At 2.30 the bell went, and we again assembled in the lecture-room for a further two hours. The morning lecture would be continued, or various officers would be called on to read from Marxist books. After roll call at six, there was "group study" and "discussion" in the squad-rooms, with an interpreter presiding. We tried to make these as farcical as we dare.

The chief political commissar was a little man called Comrade Sun—a fanatical young Marxist speaking fairly competent English. He would enter, gaze disdainfully upon the raffish, murmuring multitude and cry out in his high-pitched voice "Keep silence". Other comrades patrolled the corridors, noting those who paid no attention, or who dozed or scoffed. Sometimes Sun would order an officer (preferably a senior rank) to stand up and give a résumé of the lecture or reading. In this way, bad marks could be totted-up against you. Once he caught me napping:

"Davies, stand up."

I rose.

"What is your opinion of the chapter we have just read?" (It was from William Z. Foster's *Outline History of the Americas*.)

Long pause, then:

"I'm afraid I was not listening."

"Why not?"

"Well, I'm a British P.O.W. and I have other interests than American history."

Silence—

"You will pay attention. You must correct your attitude."

Ponderously—

"I confess my crime."

"Sit down."

Sometimes we were issued with paper and pencil and faced with examination papers to gauge our "political self-consciousness". Typical questions were:

"Give the reasons for the ever-deepening crisis of world-capitalism."

"What is the programme of socialism?"

"Is peaceful co-existence between the two different social systems possible?"

"Why does the Soviet Union head the World Peace Camp?"

"Who is the unjust aggressor in Korea?"

"Give Lenin's five contradictions within capitalism."

"Say why the triumph of world-socialism is inevitable."

A number of those who gave unsatisfactory answers would be called before Commander Ding to explain themselves and learn the truth. These occasions tended to degenerate into bullying sessions. I was summoned to one. Ding informed me that as I was a "religious man" I should write the truth, but I had written a slander against the "peace-loving people". I was warned. An American sergeant had written that "the Reds" were responsible for the war. He would not retract. Sun yelled at him: "You are just a tool of the warmongers." The big sergeant shook his cropped head like a bull at bay. He got 21 days solitary.

Even the tireless Sun found us incorrigible, and after six months the Chinese more or less abandoned this kind of indoctrination in Camp 2. Many officers captured before February 1951 had had fourteen months' incessant indoctrination of this type. Indoctrination was in no sense "voluntary". The penalty for refusing to attend Sun's lectures was confinement in a cell in a temperature of thirty below, with one blanket and two meals a day. We went, albeit "unwillingly to school". Later, when we accused the Chinese of "compulsory indoctrination" they evaded the issue by saying "We do not compel you to believe anything", and that the lectures were "Camp rules and regulations you must obey". The object was to "awaken your political self-consciousness", so that you might "Identify yourself with the broad masses of the people". Files were kept on all prisoners: men were labelled politically—progressive, backward, hostile or reactionary.

Officers were continually taken for interrogation and discussion. Extraordinarily detailed questionnaires were presented to us.

".What property do you own?"
"What is your father's income?"
"What is your wife's political affiliation?"
"Where were you educated?"
"What is your religious affiliation?"
"What were your grandparents' occupations?"
"Name three intimate friends."

We had two meals a day. Our staple food was rice and soya-beans. Once a week we had pork—one whippet-like pig among three hundred and seventy very hungry officers. Each man received one or two small squares. The pork-gravy went deliciously with our rice. Later, our diet was improved by regular issues of steamed bread, which is rather like eating blocks of tough suet pudding. "Dikons" (the Korean turnip) were ever-present the first year. Cabbage leaves and potatoes were very frequent items later. In the last year of our captivity, food improved steadily and the summer diet of 1953 contained tomatoes, greens, a few eggs, and canned meat sometimes as often as three times a week. This year, too, the Chinese began to give us a daily issue of tea.

We collected our food by squads from the kitchen in buckets and wooden boxes. In the squad rooms we placed our rice-bowls and cups round the bucket, and the "bucket-man" for the day doled out the portions.

It should be remembered that we were probably

eating better food than many Korean peasants, whom war had driven from their homes.

Each squad had a bucket and a wash-pan. From dawn we kept a fire burning under a gasoline drum full of water, and from this the squads drew their hot washing water each morning. Squad-members queued for their ablutions. Eventually the Chinese had a communal concrete bath built, holding about fifteen men.

Indoor recreations were chess, bridge, poker and incessant talking. Many remarkably attractive chess sets were carved by the prisoners out of odd chunks of wood. The Chinese later gave us regular issues of playing-cards. There was a remarkably skilled American vocal quartet. Their "Twelfth Street Rag" and "Blue Skies" set everyone swaying. King of the guitarists was "Stan". Many sat at the feet of this genial negro officer in the evening twilight outside "Chateau Stanley", while he soothed away sorrow with his warm voice and agile fingers. Summer recreations were volley-ball, netball, American baseball and soccer. Pacing the parade ground was always popular, either alone with one's thoughts, or with special friends. Impromptu concerts were also arranged. We made an effort to conduct modern language classes, literary, art and mathematical sessions. All this was from memory, and some mis-information was probably absorbed.

In late November, 1951, a group of Americans who had been in North Korean hands since capture in July, 1950, were admitted to our compound. They were scraggy and dirt-grimed, clad in rags, and some of them had skin diseases through no fault of their own. They had had a rough time, and were greatly relieved to come under Chinese jurisdiction. Only

*Panorama of Camp No 2 from the house on the hill
Aug/52.*

6. A general rear view of Camp 2, from the "House on the Hill" (where the senior officers lived until October 16th, 1952).
An original sketch by Major Guy Ward, T.D., R.A., done in August 1952.

7. The "House on the Hill", Camp 2. Here the senior officers lived until the camp was split into two compounds.
An original coloured sketch by Major Guy Ward, T.D., R.A., dated July 1952.

*outside the House on the Hill Camp
July/52*

6. Beyond the tall poplars, which I always called "The Seven Sentinels", lay the village and "high street" of Pi-chong-ni. The camp was enclosed with fencing and barbed-wire, with sentry posts at four places. The parade and recreation ground in front was about 85 yards by 40 yards. In the extreme left of the sketch lies the H.Q. of the Chinese Company (not Camp) Commander.

To the right of the black-trunked tree on the slope is the camp-kitchen. The long Korean schoolhouse had plastered clay and wattle walls, floor-boards, and a corrugated iron roof. It was divided into twelve squad-rooms in which lived, until October 16th, 1952, over three hundred prisoners. The schoolhouse was about 80 yards long. At the extreme right wing is the camp library, about 60 feet by 20 feet, used as our chapel on Sundays, and for political indoctrination on week-days. Here Colonel Carne underwent his "people's trial" on February 8th, 1952.

The lower-roofed building adjoining the library is a latrine. In the bitter winter, urine and excrement froze in blocks, and cleaning the latrine meant hours of chipping for us. Still it was better than in summer—no flies!

7. The "house on the hill", overlooking Camp 2, was rather attractive with a fine fluted roof. It commanded a superb view down the valley, which looked lovely in the spring when the tender green of the rice-shoots covered the stinking paddy-fields. A path ran down the steep slope into the general compound, and between roll-calls there was free access both ways to all prisoners.

In this sketch prisoners are seen playing bridge and simply chatting. All are wearing blue cotton prisoners' trousers, two are wearing the sack-like white shirts issued by the Chinese. Temperature about 90-95°.

the strongest had survived their early march north under "the Tiger", a fanatical North Korean major.

They had been with the civilian group, and told us wonderful stories of the French nuns; of Bishop Cooper; Commissioner Lord of the Salvation Army, and Monsignor Quinlan. One spoke of the Sisters trying to wash prisoners' soiled underclothes in the snow; another of his secret baptism by the Bishop—a service interrupted four times as the Korean guard passed to and fro, to keep the prisoners from talking; another of Monsignor's unfailing gaiety.

"Ah'm tellin' yuh, man, yuh sure got religion with these guys," said a young lieutenant from the deep South. It was a fine tribute.

One night, the tall American doctor who had come in with this group told me a story of Commissioner Lord. "We were dead beat. Another terrible day's march lay ahead. The men were lying cold and half-starved in the lousy shacks waiting for the command to get going. A lot of those guys thought they couldn't make it—they felt they'd had it. Suddenly old Commissioner Lord appeared in the doorway of our shack. He seemed very confidential about something.

" 'Boys,' he said, 'Boys, I've got news for you—great news—listen.' We all took notice. We all thought 'What's with this guy?' That old Commissioner, why he just stood among us and said, 'The Lord is my shepherd; I shall not want,' and he went right through that psalm, like it was God's personal message to us. Chaplain, I'm telling you, you could *hear* the silence. I never felt so moved in all my life. Then the guards came—it was get going or die. Those men rose like they had new strength. Can't tell you where they got it from. They

5

marched and stuck it out. 'The Lord is my shepherd . . .' I shan't ever forget that morning."

When these prisoners first joined us they were gaunt, silent, brooding men afraid to raise their voices.

It was marvellous, almost ludicrous to see them fatten, and to hear them become chatty men again, able to crack a joke, able to laugh and sing. They felt grateful to the Chinese for food, fresh clothing and material benefits which by comparison with North Korean prisoner-of-war standards seemed amazingly good.

In 1951, our Chinese captors decided to give us facilities to observe the Christmas Festival. We were to organize a camp concert, decorate the camp, have a special dinner, and—most important of all—hold our religious services. It was to be a holiday, and this meant a temporary cessation of the compulsory lectures and study-groups on Marxism and Soviet Communism.

There was a spirit of expectancy abroad, an illusory sense of impending freedom. Small parties left the compound, under armed guard, to gather fir branches and select a Christmas tree from the snowy mountainsides rising steeply from the bowl in which the prison camp lay. Concert rehearsals went on in the drab, cold lecture-room beneath portraits of Marx, Engels, Lenin, Stalin, Mao Tse-Tung, Slansky (still in favour!), Harry Pollitt and the rest. Rumours of chicken for dinner, bread, a packet of cigarettes each, peanuts, tea and "saki" filled the air. This promised some relief from the eternal rice, beans and "dikons".

As chaplain, I was negotiating the religious side of things with the camp authorities. To our great joy they were to give us, as a special concession, a loaf of bread and a bottle of grape-wine for Holy Communion—our first Communion since capture for some of us, a year ago. I had to write out, word for word, the prayers, carols and Scripture readings, even to the extent of the "Our Father" and Apostles' Creed, for Chinese censorship—a most exact, scrupulous and often fantastic thing, motivated by the fear of political ribalding or cryptic lampoons on Marxism and Mao Tse-Tung. On the morning of Christmas Eve, we were given the use of the mimeograph machine from Chinese H.Q. in the village, with which to print the approved carols.

Christmas Communion was at 8 a.m. in the lecture-room. The altar was a table draped with blue curtaining material, surmounted by a beautifully-carved Celtic Cross. This had been made by Colonel Carne from local Korean stone. His implements were two large nails and a primitive hammer. He spent day after day in the bitter December weather, patiently rubbing smooth the sides of his Cross on the concrete steps of the Korean schoolhouse in which we lived. He presented it to me for use in our religious services. This Eucharist was its initiation into the service of the Church of the Captivity. It became a symbol of endurance and of conquest, of Christian faith "in spite of dungeons".

The congregation of some ninety-five British and American officers stood in the ice-cold room while the Eucharistic celebration proceeded. From the window a Chinese guard peered in open-mouthed for a few moments. Kneeling on folded blankets, the faithful received the Sacrament. For Colonel Carne it was his first and last Communion in captivity. Our chalice was a green Chinese metal cup, our paten a British mess-tin.

Vestments I had none, save my blue prisoner's uniform. At the end of the service my fingers were so stiff with cold I could hardly handle the vessels on the altar. Looking at the pictures of the dialectical materialists gazing down on the scene, St. John's words came to my mind, "This is the victory that overcometh the world, even our faith."

At 11 a.m. we had Morning Service with carols and lessons, attended by more than two hundred and fifty prisoners. They sat, like Orientals on the bare floor-boards. As I read the final lesson—"In the beginning was the Word . . ."—the Camp Commander, Ding, came to the foot of the platform and began taking snapshots of the altar, of me and of the assembly. A murmur of protest arose from the congregation, but he seemed unperturbed and I continued to read the solemn words of St. John's Gospel.

In the afternoon the "saki" was issued along with peanuts. Inevitably some men got drunk, and some became violently sick. Dinner at five o'clock was a voracious meal, eaten squatting on our sleeping-mats in the squad-rooms. It was for us a Ritz affair—bread, potatoes and chicken, a meal not to be rivalled until the following Easter. The slapstick concert took place in the crowded, smoke-filled lecture-room, the church of that morning, our pathetic conviviality combating the sub-zero temperature. There were cookies, too, and black, potent "coffee" made from burnt sorghum.

So the Festival of our Redeemer's birth passed, and the atmosphere of make-believe holiday was dispersed by the harsh reality of our prisoners' life. A few days later we sat in the lecture-room while the Chinese urged us to send a greetings card to General Peng Te-Huai at the front, in gratitude for the "Lenient Policy" of the Chinese Volunteers in Korea. Their solicitations were met by a stubborn silence, and their frustration expressed itself in the removal next day of the senior American officer to solitary confinement in the windowless, unheated jail on the road. Later in the month Colonel Carne met the same fate. I was sitting with him and a small group of British officers on the afternoon of January 28 (1952), discussing life in London, when he was summoned to the Chinese H.Q. Rather more than a week later, he and several other British and American senior officers, grimy, unshaven and all looking blue with cold (the daily temperature was 30 below, and they had been in unheated cells), were brought before us into the camp lecture-room, closely guarded by soldiers with fixed bayonets. "Snake-eyes", surrounded by his eager assistants, presided over this assembly where these prisoners were accused of "subversive activities"; "plots against the camp authorities" and of "using their rank to intimidate the junior officers to prevent them learning the truth". This was in reference to the steadying leadership, example and guidance given by the Colonel, Major Harding of the Gloucesters, and the other American officers who were up for this "people's trial". After their so-called "confessions" had been read and their indictments pronounced, the officers were led away, all of them maintaining great personal dignity and self-control in peculiarly trying circumstances. Colonel Carne now entered upon his nineteen months of solitary confinement.

The next day we were issued with paper and pencil and told to record our "cognition" of what was called "the case". Many guarded and cryptic comments were sent in to H.Q. My own was, "I found the case highly instructive." The compound hummed with impotent indignation and disgust. This was not mollified by a reminder of the paradoxical nature of our captivity given us by a Chinese official in the familiar lecture-room, who prefaced his address with the incredible words, "Liberated officers of the American and British Armies . . ."

CHAPTER SIX

The Lenient Policy

THE keynote of the Chinese Communists' attitude to their prisoners-of-war is the celebrated "Lenient Policy". On several occasions Commander Ding gave long lectures on this theme. We were sometimes faced with questionnaires about it. The subject was always cropping up.

It was a freezing afternoon in January, 1952, when for several hours "Snake-eyes" first expounded it in my hearing. We squatted before him on the floor, chilled and hungry, to learn once again the lesson of Chinese leniency. Big Wong interpreted. This is the gist of his discourse, many phrases of which ring as clearly in my ears to-day as when I first heard them.

"From the very first days of our People's Liberation Army we have carried out the Lenient Policy towards war-prisoners. It is not something first invented in the Korean War, but a policy rooted in our People's Army from the beginning.

We know you believe in the Geneva Convention and the Red Cross. These are instruments of bourgeois idealism which it is impracticable to carry out, as we believe you will eventually realize. Moreover, they are used by the imperialists and capitalists to cover their evil plans. Our Lenient Policy is perfectly sufficient for all your reasonable needs. It is a sincere policy, based on principles of humanitarianism, equality and international law. When you really understand it, you will no longer be critical of it.

You have come here as dupes of the imperialists, the warmongers, and the Wall Street big-shots, who have forced you to come from your homes, and your loved ones to fight their dirty war for blood-soaked profits against the Korean people. We could justly kill you as war-criminals, and enemies of the peace-loving people of the world. But we know you are only dupes and tools of the warmongers. You have been liberated now. We shall not harm you. No, true to our Lenient Policy we shall deliberately preserve your lives and help you to learn the truth. Later on you will self-consciously realize this and thank us. We extend leniency towards you and help you.

Some of you accuse us of not taking care of you, and of letting our prisoners die. We tell you many of your men fell sick and died because they could not eat our type of food. Also, they had many bad diseases, brought on by vice, which are hard to cure. The American 'planes, too, caused great damage, and food supplies could not get through. Some of you think you should be living in luxurious conditions like an hotel in the Pentagon. We did not invite you to come to Korea to slaughter and rape the innocent, peaceful Korean people.

Now you are here we do our best for you, and we give you this opportunity to open your eyes and

see the truth. You should be grateful. This is our
Lenient Policy. But many of you care only for
dollars and girls' legs, and do not wish to study hard
and learn the truth. We think there are four types
of men among you:

First, there are the righteous, progressive men
who are self-consciously learning the truth. These
men are our friends, international friends, who are
struggling free from the toils of the warmongers, and
gaining solidarity with the peace-loving people of the
world. We shake their hands.

Secondly, there are the semi-righteous men who
are uncertain. They are swayed by every wind that
blows. They incline this way and that way. They listen
to both sides, but cannot make a self-conscious decision.
They are basically good men, but too weak. We want
to be friends with them, but they cannot make up
their minds to accept the truth.

Thirdly, there are the men who are easily influenced
by the bad men. These are they who believe all the
slanderous things, and who are afraid of the bad men
and easily intimidated by them into closing their
minds against the truth.

And fourthly, there are the bad men who are basically hostile to us, and who do their best to influence
all the other prisoners against us. These are the real
enemies of the people, the hired tools of the Wall
Street warmongers, the absolute reactionaries, members of the capitalist, ruling clique.

Most of you are basically righteous men, and we
hope you will learn the truth, but there are a few of
you who are the real enemies of the peace-loving
people, and who wish to organize subversive activities

against the camp authority, and disrupt the study programme. These men think they are clever—little Carnes, little Brownes—but they will find they cannot outwit the powerful and intelligent C.P.V. Our Lenient Policy is not limitless. It cannot be extended for ever to those who are deliberate reactionaries with a hostile attitude towards us.

So we remind you again of the Lenient Policy of the Chinese People's Volunteers. We give you warm clothes for the Korean winter; we feed you; we give medical attention and regular inoculations; we look after you; we have even been known to return sick prisoners to your lines; we give you full religious freedom. If you have a conscience at all you must see how lenient we are to you.

I am not a Christian, and I do not know all your religious beliefs, but I *do* know it says in the Bible you should have a good conscience. Ask your chaplain, he will tell you. So if you really are Christians, you should have a good conscience towards us, and honestly and conscientiously appreciate our Lenient Policy. Your religion says men with a bad conscience go to Hell. You should self-consciously examine yourselves and consider our leniency to you, and adopt a good attitude to us and drop a hostile attitude.

At Panmunjom the American imperialists and their running-dogs and lackeys, the British capitalist ruling clique, are holding up the peace talks. In the imperialists' prison-camps they are torturing, starving and killing the Korean and Chinese prisoners, but we will remain calm and will never torture or kill you. You are safe with us. We shall always self-consciously carry out the Lenient Policy and thus shall continue to give you the chance to study and learn the truth, and see how your leaders are catching the people in a web of lies and preparing to extend the Korean conflict, and unleash a third world war."

The basis of it all was the preservation of the prisoner's life so that he might "learn the truth", as his captors saw it, be converted, and join the ranks of "the people". It seemed to me a kind of political system of salvation, parallel with the Christian one.

We prisoners were given every encouragement to study and "learn the truth". There were pamphlets, Communist newspapers and most of the works of Marx, Engels, Lenin, Stalin and Mao Tse-Tung in good English translations. This was apart from the daily indoctrination classes, which occupied many hours of our time. "Peace doves" and other emblems were displayed in our camp, and we were often shown films of peace rallies in China, Eastern Germany and "the People's Democracies", and huge demonstrations against the "Wall Street dominated United Nations". We were invited to discuss and ask questions freely, and it was formally laid down that "any prisoner adopting a sarcastic attitude to the progressive students can be severely punished".

One day we were crowded into the lecture-room to discuss our "cognition of the Lenient Policy". No one would speak. Twenty minutes passed. The Chinese grew restive and embarrassed. A stubborn silence reigned. An American Army doctor, William Shadish, was called on to give his opinion. He would not express one, and remained standing stolidly. He was taken over to H.Q. for a grilling, which lasted for some hours. He was asked to "confess his hostile attitude", and to admit to them that most of the prisoners who died in the first grim winter of the captivity died from syphilis, and venereal complications brought on by their own misdeeds. He steadfastly refused to admit this, or to sign any document. He was returned later in the day after much abuse and bullying, and with a severe warning hanging over his head.

The rest of us were given a question sheet containing the words: "Haven't you received any lenient treatment at all? Give your cognition."

Men who had survived the early prison conditions of 1950-51 retained many bitter memories of that gruesome period, and to them the "Lenient Policy" seemed a sham, a political device brought out later, and necessitated by the progress of the peace talks. To others, no doubt, captured towards the end of 1951 and afterwards, the Chinese attitude to their prisoners seemed fairly reasonable, and even, on occasions, surprisingly magnanimous.

"Self-criticisms" played a big part in our lives. These were usually read out by the offending prisoner in the presence of us all. I shall never forget one burly American major, with guards at his elbow, criticizing himself before us for misusing his little green notebook—"So kindly given me by the Chinese People's Volunteer Forces in Korea that I might take political notes and learn the truth. Instead I confess I have used it for rolling cigarettes, for drawing, for latrine paper, for compiling bridge scores, for writing out food recipes and" (a heavy pause) "for doodling. For this I sincerely and deeply criticize myself." It was a masterpiece.

The strangest revelation of all was the morning when Tien, number one company interpreter, assembled us and invited us to criticize him freely for his past actions. He laid himself open to a real barracking, and he certainly got it from the "old boys" of the 1950-early 51 period at Pyuktong. They told him he was just a "stupid little schoolboy with no real experience of men or the world" and that he suffered "from a deep-rooted inferiority complex which made him vindictive". He took it like a lamb, I must say, but I'm afraid I have to record that two of those who spoke most freely at this bizarre session did spells on other charges in the frozen jail before that winter was out. One of them said later, "Yeah, Mao sees all, knows all, takes all. You gotta remember that, comrade."

I think the Chinese considered our conversion by means of the "Lenient Policy" a feasible project, and were genuinely puzzled by our stubborn allegiance to our own ways of life and thought. They could not understand our sense of humour. Once we organized a "Crazy Week". Men played at aeroplanes in the compound; Chinese squad-leaders coming to root us out at 6.30 on a dark winter's morning found us sitting solemnly playing bridge by candlelight with no cards; one officer went everywhere for a day, even to Chinese H.Q., on an imaginary motor-bike complete with noises; another shaved his head like a billiard-ball and wore a feather at roll-call, swearing he was "blood brother" to a Red Indian chief who was "one of the peace-loving people of the world". After roll-call once, we stayed in the compound in a big tight-packed circle, looking at something in the centre. The Chinese fidgeted anxiously for five minutes, and then curiosity overcame them. There was nothing there. We broke up in awesome silence, and walked away leaving them aghast. Of course, there were repercussions. The "Lenient Policy" didn't extend to "making the joke". "Crazy Week" was exposed as a subversive plot against the camp authority; its ringleaders were tried and convicted to solitary confinement, and severe threats were issued. "Crazy Weeks" were amusing distractions, but the Chinese later hit hard and tended to single out the Senior Officer, American or British, for special treatment.

Naturally, the idea of "leniency" with its implication that we were war criminals, was distasteful to us. The "Humane Policy" would have sounded better. The Chinese, however, stuck to their guns to the bitter end, and doubtless regarded their handling of the war prisoners taken by them in the Korean campaign as a triumph of the "Lenient Policy".

It is very true that the "Lenient Policy" did not extend beyond the barbed wire. When you were taken from the compound you "got it rough". Colonel Schwable, for instance, has related at the court of inquiry into his strange case how he was "subjected to the new method of breaking a human being down". He claims he was consistently degraded and humiliated, reduced to animal level, wallowing in filth, until faced with the choice "confess you waged germ-warfare or be killed". He expected physical torture; he got "brainwashing". Some men got both, nor did rank affect the Chinese. Fusilier Derek Kinne, G.C., has told to a wide public how he underwent both physical punishment and "brainwashing" of the severest type.

It would appear that the *raison d'être* of the "Lenient

Policy" was the attempt to persuade the prisoner to accept the Communist teaching. Recalcitrance on his part, or "a hostile attitude" was evidently considered a disqualification for further "leniency".

CHAPTER SEVEN

Church of the Captivity:
My Parish Behind Barbed Wire

Our Chinese captors gave in the officers' camp, No. 2, a strictly limited measure of religious toleration that cannot be called, as their propaganda claimed, "Religious Freedom".

It is true that they forbade outright certain services, or forced us to suspend their further observance. It would be untrue, however, to say that in Camp No. 2 they physically interrupted any particular religious service while it was in progress, or that they of set policy deliberately confiscated religious books. It is even true to say that they gave help in the provision of religious facilities.

On the other hand, it must always be remembered that the Red Cross was never allowed by the Chinese to serve us in the prison camps, and that therefore I, as chaplain, was permanently deprived of religious vessels and ecclesiastical vestments, and my fellow-prisoners deprived of Bibles, prayer books and other religious literature. How we overcame this difficulty I shall relate later. Had the Red Cross been allowed to supply us, the religious picture would probably have been very much rosier, and a more normal church routine might have been established.

8. Prisoners' sleeping and general living quarters, Camp 2.
An original sketch by Major Guy Ward, T.D., R.A., dated June 1952.

9. The Camp Kitchen, Camp 2. Food was prepared here for more than 300 officers and sergeants.
An original sketch by Major Guy Ward, T.D., R.A., dated July 1952.

8. Down the centre runs an aisle, on each side of which straw-matting is laid. The prisoners' blankets can be seen, stacked along the wall. Men slept, feet to the aisle, shoulder to shoulder. In winter delightfully fuggy and warm, in summer . . . !

Along the wall in Major Ward's sketch there are ten sleeping berths indicated. In the left-hand corner prisoners are playing chess with home-made chessmen. Other prisoners are reminiscing about the "good old days".

Sleeping bunks were not built for us by our captors until six months prior to our release.

9. On the left the squads' rice boxes can be seen stacked. A squad representative collected his squad's box at meal-times, twice each day, on the call "CHOW".

Underneath the big rice and soup pots set in the clay containers, can be seen the fire-boxes. Roaring fires burned all day, heating the food and boiling our drinking water.

A staff of sixteen prisoners worked in the kitchen, and had their quarters adjoining. The place was often filled with acrid smoke, and the cooks' eyes became sore and almost permanently inflamed.

On Sunday evenings I always held an informal church service for the kitchen staff in their quarters. The Chinese told me the service must not last more than fifteen minutes, and no more than twelve men could be present. We often stretched a point, however!

As late as May, 1953, the Chinese would not countenance our request for an application, through Chinese
sources, to the U.N. negotiators at Panmunjon for Bibles,
hymn books, rosaries, Holy Communion vessels and
vestments. General Wang Yang-Kung, G.O.C. all
prisoner-of-war camps, announced at Pyuktong on
May 23, 1953, that "the small items you need for the
services will be made available". What these "small
items" were may be inferred from previous Chinese
presentations to me, on my repeated requests, and
sometimes in a humiliating and provocative manner,
of candles; grape-wine and baked bread for Communion
(on five occasions in two years); blue curtaining material
and paper for the cyclo-styling of Christmas carols,
and a tiny selection of hymns. As late as June 13, 1953,
a categorical "No" was given to my formally written
request—by no means the first one—for facilities for a
monthly celebration of the Holy Eucharist.

I was not allowed to visit the other ranks for religious
ministrations, in spite of requests from me and, as I
learned later, from the men themselves. In Camp
No. 1, for instance, there was no communal religious
observance whatsoever. The men had asked for me at
Christmas and Easter, and had later grown apathetic
in face of Chinese refusals. An American captain, there
in June, 1953, was appalled to find no Sunday observance.
British and American officers also assure me that from
May, 1951–October, 1951, at Chong-Song Prison Camp,
requests for public, organized religious worship were
refused by the Chinese. When I arrived at that camp
on October 27, 1951 (a week after the officers had
gone up to Camp 2 on the Yalu River) it is certainly
true that outward religious observance on Sunday, or

6

any other time, was forbidden. At that time, too, Christian rites at prisoners' burials were discouraged, and it was forbidden to erect crosses over graves. The Chinese said that this sign was "offensive to the Korean people".

I, personally, have no sensational account to tell of all-out atheistic "religious persecution". The technique was more one of frustration and mental harassment. When I first told the story to a well-known Army personality, he said: "It illustrates so clearly the tricky nature of Oriental Marxist dialectic."

There was a degree of religious toleration—yes, but it was a toleration so hedged about with prohibitions, warnings, accusations, mental harassment, censorings, punishments, of givings here and takings away there, that to dignify it with the name of "Religious Freedom" would be farcical. I believe that I have seen in a microcosm the pattern of what is happening to the Church in all the Communist-dominated countries.

In the prison camp we saw on a small scale the policy adopted in lands within the Communist orbit: the technique of isolation of the victim; his "confession"; his self-accusation; his apparent acquiescence in his own sentence. Prominent Church leaders and political personages have been exposed to this, and some have succumbed.

V.I. Lenin's words, spoken before the State Duma in 1909, appear to provide the clue:

"The philosophical basis of Marxism is dialectical materialism, which is absolutely atheistic and resolutely hostile to all religion. Marxism has always regarded the modern religions and Churches, and all religious organizations, as instruments of bourgeois reaction that serve to defend exploitation and drug the working-class. We must know how to fight religion."

The Church of the Captivity was the worshipping community and fellowship of the baptized within the prison camp. It was my privilege to be their priest: chaplain to the Church of the Captivity. Our corporate worship was offered to God in the camp lecture-room. Mostly this room echoed with the discordant sound of political indoctrination or "people's trials", but from time to time voices of prayer and praise rose within it.

It was a drab, cold room, about 60 by 20 feet. On one side it was flanked by a corridor, along the stretch of which you looked in through glass panes, on the other side by a wall with wide windows looking over the camp parade-ground. Portraits of the world's Communist leaders hung there until secretly torn down one night by desperado prisoners in March, 1952. A big "trial" developed out of this. Later that year, the walls were covered by lurid "Germ Warfare" posters, and Chinese guards were placed in the lecture-room day and night. At our times of worship we placed Colonel Carne's little stone cross on a rough wooden table, draped with a length of blue curtain, and flanked it with rice-bowls full of wild-flowers in season, and with candles when we had them. Everyone gathered round, either standing or squatting on the floor-boards, or sitting on blocks of wood.

Our services were simple, consisting of three well-known hymns, corporate confession, absolution, two Scripture readings, a psalm recited by me, prayers and sermon. We had one Book of Common Prayer (with English Hymnal), and several New Testaments. Every month the Chinese issued us with quite big sheets of cigarette paper. Men donated this precious paper for religious use and gradually we made over forty little hymn books, using cigarette paper and odd squares of cardboard, held together at the spine by pieces of cast-off material sewn with infinite patience. People would volunteer for copying the words.

Every service closed with the hymn:

> "Faith of our fathers, living still
> In spite of dungeon, fire and sword."

It seemed symbolic of a prisoner's defiant faith in face of Marxist captors.

From the time of my entry into P.O.W. Camp 2 on the last day of October, 1951, until June 8, 1952, our public services followed a pattern. We gathered every Sunday morning (when the Collect, Epistle and Gospel were recited as part of the service), and every Wednesday evening. I also visited the cooks in their kitchen quarters every Monday evening for prayers, because most of them could not attend the public service. At Christmas and Easter we were given a small bottle of wine and a loaf of bread for Holy Communion.

It is important to note these arrangements and the dates, because they were to play a big part in my subsequent conviction by the Chinese, and solitary confinement.

In addition to these activities, I organized Confirmation groups, Bible study, choir practice and administration of Holy Baptism.

The Roman Catholic chaplain, the heroic Father

HOLY BAPTISM

• • •

. the second Sunday after the Epiphany, 20ᵗʰ Janua
2, LEONARD LEVI MOREE, AF 17225965
b.11ᵗʰ Dec. 1929. Sgt. USAF.
vas baptised according to the rites of the Church
of England in the presence of his witnesses.
Henry Xavier Metz, Staff Sgt. USAF
and
Michael Denis George Conybeare Ryan, Major
the Royal Ulster Rifles.
Signed: S.J.Davies (Revᵈ S.J.Davie
Chaplain, the Royal Army Chaplain
D.
isoner-of-War Camp No. 2, Ping-son-ni, North Korea

10. A Baptismal Certificate on Chinese cigarette-paper.

10. Six prisoners were secretly baptised by me in P.O.W. Camp 2, and the details set down on strips of Chinese cigarette-paper from our monthly issue. Several of these certificates were smuggled out of captivity.

Chinese censorship of our religious services was so wearisome and absurd, that I felt I could not risk a downright refusal on the issue of Baptism, and preferred to take the chance of being detected in clandestine "illegal religious activities".

Kapaun, had died in captivity. His flock, numbering some eighty American and British officers, met separately for Rosary and prayers conducted by an American lieutenant, Ralph Nardella, to whom the Father had entrusted this sacred task.

Among the prisoners captured prior to May, 1951, Father Emil Kapaun's name is a legend. He was a Roman Catholic chaplain of the American 1st Cavalry Division. He died on May 23, 1951, in Camp 5, worn out by dysentery and with a blood-clot in his right leg.

In the terrible conditions of winter 1950-51, before my own capture, when prisoners were dying daily in alarming numbers and the remainder were living in a sub-zero temperature, insufficiently clad and half-starved, this chaplain was an inspiration to all. Very many stories are told of his selflessness; his cheerfulness; his devotion to the sick; his hours spent washing (without soap) their soiled underclothing; his nightly rounds for prayers in the wretched, lice-infested, unheated shacks.

He was a great "scrounger" for the sick, and made many cautious raids on Chinese food supplies. Before setting out on these hazardous adventures, he would invoke the prayers of Saint Dismas, the Penitent Thief!

This heroic and gracious young priest endeared himself to all, of many varied religious allegiances. Denominational differences were no obstacle to his ministry of religious and moral comfort to his fellow-prisoners.

After Father Kapaun's death, Major Ryan held a service of remembrance. Here is what an American captain, a Baptist, wrote in the back of his tattered Bible:

"Father Emil Kapaun passed away to his heavenly reward on 23rd May, 1951, at Pyuktong. Major Joe Ryan, a British officer, who held our Protestant service on the 27 May, paid tribute to him. He said that Father Kapaun certainly did not hide his light under a bushel, but the whole manner of his everyday life shone forth to glorify our Heavenly Father."

In spite of Communist obstructive tactics, I was able to prepare nineteen American and British officers for confirmation. Six Americans were secretly baptized in the carpenter's shed in the compound. This was a tiny hut controlled by the prisoners. Here, after posting a look-out man, I used to baptize. The font was a rice-bowl flanked by lighted candles. The candidate stood between his sponsors. I used to say:

"Sorry the surroundings are not too dignified, but when you think of it getting baptized in a carpenter's shed is rather appropriate."

I issued Baptismal Certificates on cigarette paper. Some of these were brought out of captivity.

It was a great tragedy that I was never allowed to visit the other-ranks in their compounds for religious ministrations. Men did emerge, however, as religious leaders and did their best to organize worship and Bible study. Such were Rifleman Arthur Mallett, Private Albert Knott, Corporal Newsome and Corporal Bailey. Before my arrival in a P.O.W. Camp, Major Ryan had most bravely and unflaggingly continued religious services in Camp 5. Later, after removal from Camp 2, he was placed in a group of American and

British "reactionaries" and gave inspiring leadership there, conducting Bible classes and regular communal prayer in face of Chinese displeasure. More than once he underwent "solitary", and was stood in the bitter winter weather, stripped bare to the waist.

I had to submit to a religious censorship. At first this merely meant a very full, detailed account of the Christmas services. 1951. Every prayer, every carol, every Bible reading, had to be written down for scrutinization at Chinese H.Q. This included the "Our Father" and the Apostles' Creed. I managed to evade writing down the words of the Eucharistic Canon by simply stating "Here the bread and wine are consecrated for the religious purpose of Holy Communion." This formula passed the censor until 1953. Then, after Christmas, I had to write out again the "religious schedule"; my "cognition" of the services; and my "appreciation" of the help the Chinese had given. This was normal routine and was applied to all functions in the compound—social, dramatic, sporting or religious. The Chinese are great paper-lovers. All this was a great wearisomeness to the flesh.

Later in 1952 I was compelled to submit to a much stricter censorship, under which I had to give accounts of all forthcoming services *three days before the event.*

Later on this was dropped, and instead I had to hand in at the end of each month a religious report in retrospect, covering every service held, with the words of all hymns, prayers and Scripture portions. This system continued until my release after the Armistice.

I submitted to this provocative censorship for the sake of peace, fearing lest the Chinese should altogether forbid the services (as they once threatened), or remove me permanently from the compound, thus depriving the P.O.W.s of their sole chaplain.

Here are five remarkable examples of Chinese Marxist censorship.

For the American Thanksgiving Day Service (last Thursday of November) I had to submit for censorship the order of prayer. In the prayers was naturally included George Washington's famous "Prayer for the Nation". The Chinese called me to H.Q. and explained that they permitted the prayer, provided I omitted the phrase "incline the hearts of the citizens to cultivate a spirit of subordination and obedience to government". I asked why. They replied:

"In George Washington's time it was all right, but now it is the reactionary Government of Truman backed by the Wall Street warmongers, and it is wrong for men to be obedient to it."

I said:

"But you are Marxists. You do not believe there is a God. So what does it matter to you what I say in prayers?"

The interpreter replied:

"You do not understand the problem. Bad words like this give the students a bad example and arouse warmongering feelings."

Rather than mutilate the prayer, we omitted it altogether.

At Christmas, I was forbidden to organize a little shadow-mime play on the theme of "Good King Wenceslas" and the carol was struck out. Why? Because "This has a reactionary attitude to the working people. It is a story of feudal bourgeois philanthropy."

Captain Pike of the Gloucesters wrote a clever little

detective play based on *An Inspector Calls* for our Christmas concert. A family called "the Maxwells" figured in it. At H.Q., he was told by the censor: "We think this is a joke against Karl Marx. You must change this name." The play went on, but the offending family appeared as "the Rodwells". Needless to say, "Lefty" Jones *had* to go!

In May, the Roman Catholic Community sought permission from the Chinese to organize special public prayers in a novena for peace. Their representatives were called before the Company Commander:

"It is not necessary. It is the American imperialists and warmongers at Panmunjom who prevent peace in Korea. Your prayers do no good. When the warmongers have a sincere attitude there will be peace."

The novena was forbidden.

The song, "Little Grey Home in the West" was to be sung at a camp concert. The Chinese strictly forbade it because of its lines referring to the man who wished to retire to his cottage, and "let the rest of the world go by". They maintained that this taught a reactionary, bourgeois dogma of escapist individualism. The censor said: "The man should be in the fields engaging in communal peaceful labour."

The Chinese had, all things considered, been helpful over the Christmas services in 1951. They had given paper for carol printing, candles, bread and wine. Then came the trouble over the greetings telegram to General Peng Te-huai, Supreme Chinese Commander in Korea. Colonel Browne, the Senior American Officer, and Colonel Carne were removed into jail, tried, forced to "confess" in public and sentenced to long periods of solitary confinement. The peace negotiations down at

Panmunjom had foundered for the time, the hope of a Christmas settlement had evaporated and the Chinese doubtless felt "browned-off". This was fully reflected in their changed attitude to us in the prison camp.

Hitherto, I had received every Sunday afternoon a pass to visit the little makeshift camp hospital, which was situated in a row of Korean cottages, about fifty yards beyond the barbed wire compound. I was taken past the sentry, and allowed into the hospital to visit the sick officers for the space of about half-an-hour.

This was a privilege I, and the sick, valued greatly. I used to talk to them for a little about their friends in the compound and about any home-mail received. I used to convey verbal messages of greeting and good-will. That was all. After that I read the Gospel of the Day to them, commented upon it, said prayers and blessed them. Usually, there were about ten patients, all lying on the floor wrapped in blankets, or sitting against the wall. It was a weekly half-hour full of consolation for me and for them.

The Sunday after the "trial" and "confessions" of Colonels Carne and Browne and several other senior officers, I reported to Company H.Q. for my hospital pass. The Chinese interpreter said:

"No, to-day you cannot go."

"Why is this?"

"It is not necessary. Go back."

"I do not understand. The sick men will be very sad."

"You will be told. The Camp Commander say you cannot go."

"Does this mean never go again?"

"I do not know. Go back."

The date was Sunday, February 11, 1952. From that

time until my release on September 5, 1953, I was never again permitted to visit the sick in the camp hospital.

On Thursday morning, February 28, I was summoned to Camp H.Q., outside the compound. A small, scar-faced Chinese hunchback conducted the business.

"You must write a report of all religious activities and give in detail all services in the camp."

An hour later this was completed. I gave a true and faithful account of all services and activities.

I asked for permission to visit the hospital again. My interpreter replied:

"I think it is not necessary. Camp Commander say you cannot go. We have been informed you were Browne's correspondent."

Here was a blow, quick and unexpected.

"What do you mean? I do not understand what you say."

"We know you carried secret messages from Browne to the hospital, to incite the sick men against the Camp Authorities."

"This is ridiculous. I deny this—it is not true."

"We are Marxists: we wait until we know all the facts. Then we take action. You cannot deceive us. We know all in your camp."

A little later in this session it was oilily suggested to me that information had been given regarding my use of the religious services as a cloak for political activity. I felt as though a net were closing round me.

"Bring these informers before me now in this room and ask them to repeat their charges in my presence."

"It is not necessary. We just warn you. You must

self-consciously correct your attitude and sincerely criticize yourself. We shall watch your actions. We know all in your camp. Every month I call you here for religious report."

The interview ended. The little hunchbacked "Minister of Religious Affairs" accompanied me to the sentry-post at the entrance to the compound. He was polite and offered his hand, smiling. But the seeds of the idea were implanted in my mind—you are a suspect; you are being watched; religion is a cloak for politics; criticize yourself.

11. The Pagoda.

n original coloured sketch by Major Guy Ward, T.D., R.A. Done in No. 1 Company Compound (*dated July* 1952)

11. The pagoda stood on a slope within the wire, overlooking Camp 2. It was a favourite place for lounging in the hot summer months, and a rendezvous for sun-bathers, several of whom can be seen in Major Ward's sketch.

I frequently held Confirmation Classes here, usually at 8 in the lovely cool summer mornings, before breakfast.

After the camp was split into two compounds, the Chinese placed the pagoda out of bounds beyond the barbed-wire, boarded its sides and used it for a potato dump. We missed it greatly.

CHAPTER EIGHT

A Gathering Storm

As I write, I have before me on my desk a small piece of crinkled brown paper, some 5 by 3 inches, covered with dates and apparently meaningless scribble, including the details of six secret baptisms. This tiny scrap of paper contains the material on which I shall draw in my reconstruction of the extraordinary religious troubles in Camp No. 2. The little document was an incriminating one from the Chinese point of view. It was smuggled ingeniously by an American officer through the "shakedowns" and out of captivity, finally reaching my bank from an American address.

After my arrival in Camp 2, I commenced my duties as chaplain to the Church of the Captivity without consulting the Chinese. They knew my status by this time; public services had been held at Camp 5 for some months; we made no effort to conceal what we were about. It seemed to me quite unnecessary to beg our captors' permission to hold our Christian gatherings. They did not interfere, and church routine continued quietly, but not secretively. In mid-November, while we were up the valley hauling wood, the small hunch-backed Chinese official, with whom I was later to have so many dealings, said to me:

"You are the man who organizes religious services and prayers in the camp."

"Yes."

"Why you do this?"

"Because I am a chaplain, and therefore I lead the men when they say prayers."

He smiled non-committally and said no more.

The church services openly continued on Sundays, Wednesday evenings and Monday evenings (for the kitchen staff). There was no interference. On the contrary, as I have related, the Chinese gave permission for an American Thanksgiving Day service, the last Thursday of November, and Christmas services. These were heavily censored, but Chinese help was given in providing facilities. From Christmas, 1951, onwards the religious troubles may be likened to a slowly gathering storm, which reached its climax in my removal from the compound into solitary confinement during August, 1952.

In March, 1952, I again tackled the authorities, seeking permission to renew my short Sunday afternoon visits to our sick. Previously I had been accused of acting as "Browne's correspondent" between compound and hospital. This time the objection changed. I was told:

"We have made independent inquiries among the sick men. They agree with us your visit is not necessary. The Commander says you cannot go. You must not ask us again."

I replied:

"I cannot believe this. I am sure our sick men want me to visit them every Sunday."

"You say we lie?"

"I do not say you lie. I say there is a mistake. Your

cognition is wrong. There is a misunderstanding."
(Cognition is a favourite Chinese Marxist word.)
"Go back."
"I wish to speak to Commander Ding myself."
"It is not necessary. Go back."

Each morning at this time we were taken out under
guard for a mile exercise walk at 7.30. This took us
past the hospital. One of the stronger patients was
standing at the entrance. As always, there was much
yelling, catcalling and banter from the marching
prisoners. I managed to get the substance of my hospital troubles across to him, and why I was not allowed
to visit. He was amazed:
"It's all bloody nonsense, padre. We'll get cracking,
anyway, from this end."
I learned later that the patients wrote an appeal to
Chinese H.Q. for me to resume my visits, urging Commander Ding to allow me to carry out my duty as a
chaplain. In reply, the Commander's personal aide
visited the hospital, and informed the patients that
if they wanted to be religious the Commander was
very pleased. They had complete freedom to say their
prayers, and the Commander was fully prepared to
send them a Bible if they lacked one. Never again
was I allowed to visit the hospital.
Fourteen months later, on May 23, 1953, at Pyuktong,
General Wang Yang-Kung made the following pro-
nouncement (I quote verbatim from the written English
report the Chinese circulated among us). He was
replying to the camp's request that I should again
be allowed to visit our sick.

"It is unnecessary for the chaplain to go there praying for the patients, since it is well-known that sickness can only be cured by medical treatment. Praying can do nothing to it, but only affect the order in the hospital."

Here was a judgment at once provoking and evasive: it missed the point while being semi-plausible. I have always considered it a masterpiece in the dialectics of frustration.

I must add that our doctors, captured with us, were not allowed officially to practise in the camp, nor visit the hospital. Neither their medical advice nor their co-operation were invited by the Chinese. They were "bourgeois practitioners", and were forbidden medical instruments. They were, of course, a tremendous help and comfort to us all behind the scenes, although the Chinese threatened with deprivation of medical treatment any prisoner who asked advice from our own doctors after he had seen the Chinese doctor.

As Easter approached I sent in my request to the Chinese for bread and wine. One Thursday night in the latter part of March I was summoned to H.Q. Comrade Sun talked with me. He was in a genial mood.

"Camp Headquarters will give you bread and grape-wine for your Easter festival."

"Thank you. We are very pleased."

The talk turned to germ-warfare. This was a new subject upon which our captors were increasingly dwelling.

"What do you feel?"

"I do not express an opinion."

The talk then turned to Great Britain and to queries

about the role of the Labour Party as a betrayer of the working class. I batted on the wicket:

"In Britain we believe the achievement of a really good society will come, and *is* coming, by evolution and not by revolution."

Sun said:

"This is a reformist, bourgeois view."

I said:

"It is a view most of our working people hold in Britain. Already their living standard is quite high. They do not agitate for violent revolution."

Silence. Then I asked him:

"How is Colonel Carne?"

"He is very well. Do not worry about him. He is carving something. It looks like an angel. I think maybe it is an Angel of Peace."

Then Sun said something which I remembered long afterwards when I was being accused of "illegal activities" by the Chinese, because it showed that H.Q. knew perfectly well what our religious routine was, well before Easter, 1952.

"How many men attend the mid-week service?"

"Oh, about forty or fifty. It varies—but usually about that number."

At this time, the American major whom the Chinese had appointed "chairman" of the "Daily Life Committee" and myself, were agitating for permission to be given me to pay an Easter religious visit to the officers undergoing solitary confinement in jail. Altogether we tried three formal, written requests and two verbal ones. The Chinese did not vouchsafe an answer except "It is impossible". Easter came and went, and I was not

7

allowed to visit them. This again was a severe frustration. I was told a little later:

"These men are being punished for bad deeds. Therefore they cannot have these privileges."

I replied:

"But in my·country bad men, even murderers, are allowed to see the chaplain at Easter."

They said:

"It is different. Here you are in a P.O.W. Camp."

On Good Friday we held a Service of the Passion of Our Lord. I trained a group of officers to read the Passion narrative in dialogue form, with a crowd filling in its part, after the manner of the chanting of the Passion in the Good Friday Liturgy of Holy Church. I preached to the camp. In the evening we held a devotional service with reading of St. John's Passion.

Easter Day, April 13, was a glorious, blue, warm day. The Roman Catholic community had "Sunrise Service", and I followed with the celebration of the Easter Mass. Nearly one hundred officers received Holy Communion (the camp contained about three hundred and seventy). We still had to use our Chinese metal cup for chalice, but Major Ryan's lovely little wooden paten with the words *"Ecce Panis Angelorum"* carved round the rim, was used for the first time, instead of a mess tin. Nearly the whole lecture-room was covered with violently-abusive "Germ Warfare" cartoons and slogans, so out of reverence for the Blessed Sacrament we curtained off the one free end of the room, and crowded in there for our Service. At eleven o'clock we held an outdoor Easter Service, at which I preached. A good number of Roman Catholic friends attended, having no chaplain of their own. After the service the British sang "God Save the Queen". We had just recently heard of the King's death, and I had previously called a service to offer prayers for the repose of his soul and to ask God's blessing on Her Majesty—without so much as consulting the Chinese, I may add. The Americans followed with a robust rendering of "The Star-Spangled Banner". It was immensely moving to see the compound filled with proud, stiff, motionless figures.

By one of those inexplicable *voltes-face*, the Chinese had arranged a feast for us, at which each man got a boiled egg, twenty Peking "Dragon" cigarettes, twelve candies, some peanuts, and a finger of "Saki". But they had gone further, and had hidden coloured eggs on the nearby mountainside. Chattering excitedly, like children, we were shepherded out under armed guard and for an hour allowed to roam the slopes looking for the Easter eggs. The finders got rewards. Reality seemed to recede, and fantasy took its place for the day.

That Easter evening I was summoned to Chinese H.Q. Tien, No. 1 Company's young interpreter, interviewed me. He spoke very adequate English. He was in a bitter mood.

"You have tried to deceive us. You have used the religious service as a cloak for political activities."

"But this is not true. I completely deny this charge."

"What are you?"

"I am a guest of the Chinese Volunteers."

This was rash, I shouldn't have said it. Tien flew into a white rage. He spluttered:

"Do not joke with me. What is your position? What are you now?"

"Well, I suppose I am a prisoner-of-war."

"You should self-consciously watch your conduct. Why do you incite the prisoners to sing these reactionary songs of your warmongering governments?"

"I do not understand."

"What are these songs you sing at the Easter Service?"

"You mean the National Anthem?"

"You are not allowed to sing these warmongering songs."

I asked him:

"Is the Chinese Government at war with the British Government?"

"Your Government has troops in Korea carrying on the aggressive, imperialist war against the Korean and Chinese people."

I suddenly flared up (it must have been the boiled egg that morning):

"I will not stay here and hear my country slandered by you."

He was obviously astonished at this, and strange though it must seem, he quietened down.

I was taken to another room, told to reflect on my attitude, and left alone. An hour passed. Tien reappeared with paper and ink.

"You will write your self-criticism."

I wrote a typical P.O.W. effort, saying I realized I had caused annoyance to my Chinese company interpreter; that I sang my National Anthem through love of my Motherland; and that I had intended no insult to the Chinese people.

"This is not good. It will not do," said Tien.

He conversed with another Chinese who had entered, then:

"Go back."

On Thursday, April 17 (four days after Easter), I was taken out of the compound to the Commander's H.Q. Chen Chung-Way handled the business. He was the small, hunchbacked Chinese with the badly scarred face. Chen ordered me to write a full, detailed account of the Easter religious services and "the feast we gave you". I complied. At the end of my "religious report" I wrote that the prisoners were deeply grieved at the refusal to allow me to visit the officers, Colonel Carne and rest, in solitary confinement. He was angry at this:

"This is not necessary. We already gave you the reply."

He confiscated that sheet, and I was told to rewrite the last page of my report. Then I had to write an account of the normal "religious schedule" in the camp. This I did faithfully—concealing nothing.

Chen now raised the National Anthem.

"You must deeply and sincerely confess your crime and give a guarantee."

A long argument between us began. Comrade Sun came in. After some sarcastic exchanges, he said:

"You cannot outmanœuvre us. We know that all priests are connected with politics."

Chen now threatened me that if I did not comply, the Camp Authority would no longer recognize my status as a chaplain and the religious services would be stopped.

"Reflect on your attitude, and confess."

They went, and left me under a guard for about one hour. I was faced with a problem. Should I call their bluff and stick it out, or should I comply? My main thought was—"the issue at stake is too big to gamble on. I dare not sacrifice my status as chaplain, nor risk the stopping of the services. To do so would be wrong. I am the only chaplain there is, and I have a duty to my fellow-prisoners in the compound. Great forbearance and tact are called for."

When "Scar-face" returned, I wrote a confession saying that I had now been "caused to realize" that I was wrong in having the National Anthem sung in the P.O.W. camp. I now realized that camp rules forbade it. I had sung it because of my love for my Motherland and not to insult the Chinese. I gave my guarantee as chaplain that in future I would never again cause it to be sung at a church service in P.O.W. Camp No. 2. This was accepted at last.

A new sheet was produced.

"You must give a General Guarantee."

I now had to write a dictated screed. This ran:

"*I guarantee that* I have not in the past taken part in any subversive plot or secret organization to overthrow the lawful Camp Authority of P.O.W. Camp No. 2.

I am not in the present taking part in any subversive plot or secret organization to overthrow the lawful Camp Authority of P.O.W. Camp No. 2.

I will not in the future take part in any subversive plot or secret organization to overthrow the lawful Camp Authority of P.O.W. Camp No. 2."

My past, present and future, seemed mortgaged up to the hilt.

I was tired out, very hungry, and felt as I imagine a man feels after walking across a tight-rope over Niagara Falls. My little hunchbacked mentor escorted me to the guard-post at the entry to the barbed wire compound. He smiled up at me, and his gravy-brown eyes swam viscously.

"What you tell them when you go home after the war?"

"I shall tell them the truth, Chen. Everyone will be very interested."

CHAPTER NINE

The Spider's Web

My disturbing interview with Chen Chung-Way left me with a sense of foreboding. Religious life in the camp continued without interruption from the Chinese until the arrival of a group of new interpreters and platoon leaders. I was summoned before a young newcomer called Lin. He asked me to explain to him the "religious schedule" permitted by H.Q. I told him of our services, concealing nothing, exactly as I had done in the religious reports demanded of me at H.Q. I also impressed upon him the necessity of our being given wine and bread for Whitsun Holy Communion.

A few days later I was again sent for.

"We have made inquiries and we find this is not an important festival. You cannot have wine."

"But I am the chaplain. Surely I must be asked what are the important Christian festivals?"

"It is not necessary. We made inquiries."

"But who told you it is not important? Please call for him now."

"We asked a man in your camp. Go back."

I discovered later that the man who was asked had been quite unable to tell the Chinese what Whitsun

12. The carved wooden cover of the hymn-book made by prisoners in Camp 2, and presented to me at Easter, 1953.

12. An American officer, Captain Zimmerman, carved the cover; and another American, Major Ellis, fixed the hinges, made from tin cans from the camp kitchen.

Later in the year, the Chinese took it from me to inspect it, but it was returned after a week and I was allowed to bring it out of captivity.

F28.Th. Ap17 Nanth. St. My24. 1930 - Vin "Satellising" lie to our comr (But bef. E
s. eng. midwk. Ser.!) Jn 2. Timf. impdg. intv. (Bib Cl.). Jn 8 Trinit. HQ 0730
1115 - central sn. Jn 10 Coy Cmd - I but fwd complaints (freq. of Ser. Vin ...)
Sat. Ag 9, 6-10 Twarns on rel. act "hip in bud" - ch. prac and
Groups off: Ag 12-28 College. 13 (Wed.) move t NT. 17 (Sunday)
24 Ch. 25th 1st. SC. 26th 2nd SC 9 p.m. SC iii t Guar. 27 - 9 p.m rel.
Ag 28 change y mates. Sept. 22 Ch. "harm be good" 27th returns like. 8 Oct.
req. for chair prac. Oct. 16 Split. Oct 18 rel. visits NO Sun 19 trot assess. Mon 27
20K S. rel. visits - not necess. will not accept my mtd. but will "reflect"
Xmas invit - delay right up to last min.

Jan. essay T. No Easter for jailbirds. No Hosp. visib after 8 Feb. (3 wks.
wait for NO) TR. 8 Fb. Apostles 28 My (t 29 My) Sat. Ag. 30 - 31. Sp. by
y Cma. Saluting Sept. 1. Sh to Stir. etc. Sept. 16 fence BW 17-19 onwards "their
conscience impelled them" Big photo exh. Sun 1015 - timed nicely!
May Peace Nowena - No. DW reports 52 Xmas Services HC Sam t Croch M.
M. - but no chap. Sy. Capt. HQ m Oct. march.

- Easter troubles. Ch. says Cor. Ser. "impossible in any respons".
Ap. 19. 0945 - visiting athletes - "why have they come here". Ap. 20 Req. for
chair prac. Still outstanding (Ap. 21 address new Sjts) Ap. 30. Rt Regs.
Tead, May 4 posta (dated 10 Oct. 52!) May 15 - 5.30 p.m To Hufdud
- mimeo - "logic is twisted" 4 requests 2 mags.
May 19 - 8 a.m. helpful intv. B.RWg. June 1. T gives NO
re- June 2 (PWW away!) June 2 fun t games.
June 13 - mimeo given - him write each m - NO.
N.B. as p. talks go well - attitude is friendly - "chaplain!"
McT. reports from Camp I - NO - altho' they asked for me!

Gen. Wangs summing up at Conf. 23 My. 53. "Rel. Bel" We
will stick to the policy that practiced before in the POW Camps -
no interf. w. the pr. Bel. beliefs. In the past, when the order the
the Camps was maintained and and the rules t sep. observed, there
was no restriction given to other Moslems, Cath. or Cath. rel. If
you want to conduct Ch. in Suns Vin mans explain it
to the Cry HQ and ask for permission. The small items you
need for the Services will be made available.
"It is unnecessary for a chap. to go there praying for the
patients, since sickness can only be cured by medical
treatment, praying can do nothing to it but affect
the order in the Hospital"

en L Hyslop. Bapt. 10 D. o   Epiph 6 Jan 52. James Rowe Curry. Lt. MSC
EJK 23 My 1.   b. 19/4/21. Wm A. McClain t MR
rayne A. B. Jul. 28. 1.   Epiph ii 20 Jan. Leonard Levi Morel
                               Sgt. AF. b. 11/12/25. HXM. t MR.

Ascension 52. Richd Melton Jones Sty AF b. 25/7/24
                          Wm C. McT. t HJ. Pike.

13. The scrap of Chinese toilet-paper containing in rough code the dates and material from which this book has been written. It was smuggled out of captivity. Readers are referred to the first paragraph of chapter eight.

meant. Here was a nominal Christian, unable to give a coherent explanation of Pentecost.

Lin asked for three days' notice of the Whitsunday Service, with a list of hymns, prayers and Bible readings, and an explanation in writing of what the festival meant. He told me that I would henceforth have to submit such notice of all services I might propose holding. At the end of this Whitsun report I wrote:

"It is a matter of regret and surprise to us that the Chinese forces in Korea are unable to provide their prisoners of war with one bottle of wine for the Christian Festival of Whitsun."

On Saturday evening, May 24 (1952), at half-past seven, I was taken outside the barbed wire to Camp H.Q. Chen Chung-Way sat like a spider in the centre of its web. Wong stood in the background. I stood before the table.

"Why you lie to our comrades?"

Chen's tone was harsh, his scarred face cold and hard. I felt unable to speak for a moment. I suddenly felt weak.

"Why you tell lies?"

"I do not understand. I have not told lies."

"You tell lies to Comrade Lin. You tell him we give you permission for religious services."

"Chen, I have told him exactly what I have written for you here in my religious reports."

"You tell lies."

"Bring in my religious reports I wrote for you. Put them on this table."

Wong broke in with:

"Don't be a smart guy. Comrade Chen knows what you wrote."

Chen continued:

"You used a pretext to tell Comrade Lin that we gave lawful ·authority for the religious schedule."

Wong left. Chen and I faced each other. Chen was determined to prove that I had tried to trick Lin, the new interpreter, into thinking that I had "permission" and "lawful authority" from H.Q. for our services. He now maintained that I had never had "lawful authority", but had assumed it by force of custom.

Again and again I reminded him of the religious reports I had written for him, in which I had concealed nothing. I asked him why he had allowed the services to continue in the camp for six months without let or hindrance. I asked him why he had suddenly chosen to accuse me of "lies" and "trickery". He chose a new line:

"You talk to groups of men in your camp. We have watched you. What you tell them?"

I felt the difficulty of explaining what a Confirmation Class was. I said:

"These men ask me religious questions. I tell them about Jesus Christ and the Bible."

"Did you get lawful authority?"

"No. I do not think it is necessary."

"You lie."

Round and round the talk went. I began to despair. He loosed another arrow at me:

"You satellize Chinese People's Volunteers."

I was lost. No clue seemed to offer itself.

"You mock us. The Commander is very angry. Your attitude is very bad."

Chen had his tiny pocket dictionary on his knee below the table-level. He was turning the pages feverishly, meanwhile shooting crafty glances at me. I felt a terrible urge to laugh loudly and insanely. I'd now got the clue in this bizarre crossword puzzle. It was "satirize", and the master word was "wine". They were angry with me for my remark about the lack of wine for Whitsun Communion.

"You say we cannot give wine. We can give anything that is reasonable. But your request is unreasonable. It is not necessary. We told you the answer. You satellize us."

I felt too tired to argue further, and told Chen that we had been genuinely surprised at their Whitsun refusal.

A Chinese girl-comrade came in and sat down by Chen. They conversed. Abruptly the conversation changed. Chen asked me:

"What is your opinion about the new trade agreement between your country and China?"

A few desultory exchanges of conversation followed. The atmosphere was less menacing. I was dismissed, a guard was called and I was marched back into the compound. It was ten o'clock. My squad-mates were already bedded down for the night. Questions rose from all sides in the stuffy darkness.

I knew that the storm was about to break. The following week I held a Bible class at the request of a group of American and British officers. The next day I was summoned to Company H.Q. and given a severe reprimand for organizing unlawful group activity. I protested the innocence of my action, and claimed freedom by International Law to hold religious sessions of this nature. The reply was:

"If you do, we cannot tell what you are saying. Perhaps it is political or subversive activity, and therefore you can be punished. We warn you, for your own sake, not to hold these groups."

At seven o'clock on Trinity Sunday morning, June 8, whilst the rest of the camp were still lying in their blankets (for Sunday was always a day without early roll-call), I was taken out of the compound to Camp H.Q. The little hunchbacked official confronted me.

"I explain to you the rules and regulations about religious activities in P.O.W. Camp 2."

Chen Chung-Way told me that the normal Christian day for prayer was Sunday. From now on, no other days would be permitted for religious services in the camp. The mid-week service must stop.

"We have now a policy of religious centralization. Religious activity can only take place on Sunday."

I pleaded for the Wednesday service. Chen was adamant. I said:

"Very well. I ask you to announce this to the prisoners. I cannot do so. It is your job to tell the camp you are stopping our religious service."

"We do not stop your services. We just tell you it is a policy of centralization. You must obey the camp rules and regulations."

"Do you call this 'Religious Freedom'?"

"We give you full religious freedom. You must bear the response to stop the mid-week service. You are religious leader. You must tell the men. If you spread rumours or slander our religious policy, you will be response and you will be punished."

Chen gave me ink and paper. The same old routine.

"Now you must deeply and sincerely criticize yourself for breaking the rules and regulations, and confess your mistakes in the past."

"I do not admit I have broken the regulations. I have nothing to confess."

"You have a bad attitude. You must reflect and confess."

It was past eight o'clock. Chen went for breakfast. I sat alone in the bare little room. Trinity Sunday, 1952. I prayed for help and guidance. Chen returned after about an hour. I asked for a cup of hot water to drink.

"I wish to see Commander Ding personally."

He went out. The Deputy-Commander's pregnant wife sat plucking a chicken and eyeing me curiously. On his return, Chen informed me that Ding was very busy and could not see me.

"You must write your self-criticism and confess."

He watched me intently. Again I was faced with the problem—should I call their bluff, or submit for the sake of religious peace and continuance of my ministry in the prison-camp? I decided to write something. I knew that refusal might well mean detention outside the war-prisoners' compound, and this I felt I must not risk.

My first effort was far too cautious and self-defensive to satisfy the Chinese. The second document, too, was scrapped. It was now half-past ten. Eventually I "confessed" to organizing religious services since November, 1951, "without lawful authority from the

Camp H.Q." I "realized my past mistakes", and "self-criticized myself" for not consulting the Camp Authority and obtaining legal permission. Then I had to write a "Guarantee" concerning my future religious conduct. I guaranteed to stop the mid-week service.

Tien entered. He accused me of "organizing illegal mid-week religious activities." He said:

"You told us it was a small group, but now many men come. You have used influence."

I was triumphant.

"Exactly, Tien. That's just how Christianity grew. It began with a few men and grew into a very big religion. It always grows."

Chen and Tien spoke in Chinese. Tien said:

"I could say something to hurt you very much, but we respect your religious beliefs and I will control myself."

Chen said:

"From now on Comrade Tien will deal with all religious activities. You will report to him."

I returned to the compound at half-past eleven, tired, nervy and hungry. The camp was buzzing with excitement. That Sunday evening I called for a mass attendance at Evensong in the camp lecture-room. Everyone was there. I gave a resumé of our religious life in the camp, and explained fully all that had transpired that morning, and presented my apologia to the congregation. There was tremendous moral sympathy and support. At the back of the room Chinese interpreters were unobtrusively present. The compound seethed with helpless indignation.

On Tuesday, June 10, I was summoned to Company H.Q. within the barbed wire. Tien translated for

No. 1 Company Commander. The atmosphere was easy and reasonably friendly. I was offered cigarettes.

"What do the men feel about our religious policy?"

Tactfully I explained their disappointment about the stopping of the mid-week service. Tien said:

"The Company Commander hopes you will criticize yourself before the men and admit your past mistakes. We have your confession and guarantee here."

The upshot of this meeting was that we were henceforth allowed one public service weekly, on a Sunday (either morning or evening, but not both). I was also to be allowed to visit the cooks in their kitchen quarters on *Sunday* evenings, for not longer than fifteen minutes, and provided not more than twelve men were present. My request for more frequent Communion was rejected. Monthly religious reports in detail were imposed upon me.

On Saturday evening, August 9, at half-past eight, Tien summoned me to Company H.Q. The room was dimly lit. Tien sat in the deepening shadows.

"We have studied your religious reports. Is there anything you have not reported?"

"I do not think so."

"How about the singing you organize during the week?"

"You mean our Church choir-practice?"

"Did you get permission?"

"No. It is not a religious service."

"It must stop."

I was astounded. Argument proved useless.

"You talk to groups of men during the week. What is that?"

"It is talking about religion and the Bible."

"You did not get lawful permission. It is an illegal group activity. It must stop."

"But this is fantastic . . ."

"We allow you to talk to one man on any subject, but more than one it is an illegal group activity. For your own sake, I warn you—nip it in the bud."

I made no reply, sitting there in the shadowy room, feeling the strangeness of hearing Tien use the idiom so naturally.

"So you are telling me the choir practice and all religious groups must stop. Everyone will be unhappy."

"Yes. You must criticize yourself before the men for starting these activities without lawful permission. You are to blame if they are now unhappy."

Next day, at Sunday service, I again explained to my congregation the increasing pressure of "religious freedom" exerted by our captors, and how it was becoming impossible to effect any reasonable compromise with the Chinese authorities. I likened them to the Pharisees who tried to entangle Our Lord in his talk.

On Monday, August 11, at 11 a.m., I was taken out of the compound. Liu, Ding's "Hatchet-man", a burly, heavy-jowled, sleek person with a Beau-Brummel air, interviewed me. Tien interpreted. His boyish face was sulky, his lips bitter.

"You are a trouble-maker and a bad man. You have deceived us. You organize illegal activities. You are a cunning priest. Always you try to undermine the Camp Authority and slander our religious policy. You must be punished for your crimes. If you confess now, you will get lenient punishment."

I denied all charges.

"You stirred up the men."

"I told them what you said to me at H.Q. I told them the truth."

Here was a red rag.

"The truth! You lie. You slandered our religious policy. You will be punished severely. We give you five minutes to reflect and confess."

When they returned, I was finally resolved.

"What do you say?"

"I have nothing more to say."

Liu went out, and I was stood to attention at the door of the house for about twenty minutes. Liu returned with what seemed like a charge-sheet from Camp H.Q., which Tien took.

"You have a hostile attitude to us, and have carried on illegal religious activities and slandered our policy. Follow me."

I went with Tien down the village street and was delivered into the hands of the Chinese guards.

The guard commander and a Chinese soldier with rifle and bayonet marched me to my cell. Here another Chinese official brusquely stripped me of various possessions. Everything went, even a pencil stub and some paper.

My pocket New Testament was taken and thrown spitefully to the ground. I felt as though a whip had lashed my face. I bent to pick it up, but the guard kicked it from my reach and menaced me with his bayonet. He then retrieved it and gazed at it curiously, finally flinging it again in the dirt. I begged the official for the Testament, using the Chinese word for priest and making the Sign of the Cross. He turned contemptuously away and I was thrust into the tiny cell. Two heavy wooden logs were propped against the door. I was able to peer out through the bars. Outside a guard with fixed bayonet walked slowly to and fro.

CHAPTER TEN

In Spite of Dungeons

I was in jail on charges of "illegal religious activities, and a hostile attitude". This was "Religious Freedom" with a vengeance!

My cell was six feet long by four wide. It had clay and wattle walls, and an uneven dirt floor. The cell contained a pile of foul-smelling old rubber slippers in one corner, a gasoline drum, a small tin can, and a box of lime. The floor was soaked with oil in several places. There was a heavy smell of urine, oil and well-worn gym-shoes.

The cell lay in a block facing a large warehouse. On two sides its walls adjoined other cells. Through the bars I could see the door of a cell across the way; the square in which the Chinese soldiers used to play basket-ball in the evening; and the notorious jail on the road. In the cell opposite, an American lieutenant was imprisoned. He had no look-out, and lived in perpetual darkness.

Apart from the clothes I was wearing, I was allowed a blanket and Chinese outer-coat, my cup, rice bowls and spoon. Later a well-disposed guard threw in a strip of sacking.

I bedded down the first night as well as I could. Fortunately, I was able to stretch full length, lying on my outer-coat and wrapped in my blanket. As I lay in the darkness trying to compose my thoughts for sleep, the door was flung open and, with a great flashing of torches and much chattering, the guards carried out an inspection.

The next morning I was relieved to hear the familiar voice of the Adjutant of the Gloucesters in the adjacent cell. He was calling to the guard. He had evidently been brought in during the night. I rapped on the wall and called his name. It was not long before we had made a small communication hole at the base of the clay wall and exchanged greetings. I conveniently covered the hole with the pile of rubber slippers. Tony Farrar-Hockley was just the neighbour needed for such an occasion—a soldier of resourcefulness and courage, and altogether a man of great versatility.

I soon realized there was also a prisoner in the other cell. He kept very quiet. By tapping, I drew him to the wall, and we dislodged a small chunk of clay to make a peep-hole near the floor. It was difficult to converse because the guard kept looking in through the bars and ordering me to sit upright in the middle of my cell away from the walls. We exchanged our names, however, and maintained regular communication during the whole of my confinement. Abbot was a young American Air Force corporal who had been in solitary for months because he would not "confess to germ warfare". He was extremely pleased to learn I was a chaplain, and I was able to give moral and spiritual consolation to him in sporadic conversations through our hole in the wall. By now, he had developed a black curly beard, and his sun-starved skin was white and flabby.

I soon discovered that a Gloucester company-sergeant-major was imprisoned in a tiny disused latrine at the end of the block. This was Morton, a resilient Londoner of irrepressible good humour and the guts of ten.

In another block some yards away Major "Sam" Weller of the Gloucesters was penned in a tiny coop like C.S.M. Morton's. Since the removal of Colonel Carne and Major Harding, and later of Major Ryan, of the Royal Ulster Rifles, Major Weller had taken over command of the British group in the compound. He was a fearless and resolute officer, who had given an uncompromising example of leadership in extremely trying circumstances. His reward from our Marxist captors was the same as for his predecessors: solitary confinement in semi-darkness, and in the most degrading conditions. At one stage he was made to walk to and from his cell with bare feet. Beyond him, in another tiny pen, was Gallagher, another stalwart Gloucester company-sergeant-major, a dour man with a very strong will and superb physique.

In the jail on the road six officers were confined together at this time, one of whom was Captain Pike of the Gloucesters. "Spike's" charge was that he had "incited a strike" amongst the prisoners when we were hauling wood from the barges on the Yalu. The other five were Americans. At this time, therefore, August, 1952, no less than four British senior officers, three Captains and two C.S.M.s, were known to be in jail —most of them in solitary confinement. The "Glorious Glosters" were proving a difficult crowd for the Chinese to handle.

At first light, the Chinese guard awoke us by shouting or beating on the cell-door. If he was a reasonable fellow, he would not insist on our being up much before seven. If he was out for promotion he would have us sitting bolt upright, blanket folded, by half-past five. From then until past ten o'clock we sat alone with our thoughts. It was forbidden to lie down again, and washing was entirely out of the question—no facilities were given for such a privilege. Early in the morning hundreds of flies were dozing on the walls. I used to take a rubber shoe and attempt to kill some forty or fifty each day. I believe this helped in keeping down the swarms.

If a humane guard-commander was on duty, he used to make the rounds and would arrange for us to go out, under guard, at about nine to the earth latrine. A surly guard-commander didn't bother, and nature's urgent calls went unheeded. This was a severe trial. The alternative to sheer, stoical endurance was to make use of a corner of your tiny cell. My own problem was partly solved by the fortunate presence of the box of lime. Other prisoners were not so lucky, and when outraged nature refused to fit into this inconsiderate routine, the results in a cramped space were not pleasant. Even when prisoners had bouts of dysentery, there were days when one latrine visit only was permitted. I think that some of the guards, though certainly not all, regarded this as a rather subtle joke to be played on "the Western imperialists".

It seemed an almost unendurable wait from five-thirty till mid-morning. A little after ten, breakfast arrived, with the guard enthusiastically shouting "chop-chop". It was always a bowl of sorghum and a bowl of highly-spiced egg-plant. At eleven, boiled water was brought. I was let out of my cell about three paces to wash my bowls, and get a cup of water for drinking. It was wise to fill a bowl with water for finger-washing and for moistening the face. One day, to our surprise, we got all the meat we could eat. The reason for this caused speculation for days. When I returned to the compound I mentioned this to my comrades. They all roared with laughter: "That was the lousy old mule lying dead on the road. We saw the Chinks cutting it up."

At mid-day, when it grew very hot and the Chinese bugles had blown, we were permitted to lie down and doze for an hour. By this time the flies swarmed everywhere. They covered the face and hands: they worried eyes and nose, and hovered greedily on the lips. I would lie with a handkerchief spread over my face, listening to the sound of many frustrated flies busily walking about on my linen protector. Everywhere they left their revolting traces. One day, an over-zealous young Chinese guard yelled at me for lying down after the mid-day bugle. I remained prone. He flung open the door and menaced me with his bayonet. He made me stand to attention. At that moment, the guard-commander we nicknamed "Sarge", a conscientious, good-looking young Chinaman, came along on his rounds. I had the immense satisfaction of seeing my persecutor get what can only be described as a most imperial rocket. I lay down again. Five minutes later a disgruntled guard scowled impotently through the bars, making a lewd gesture with his fingers and muttering "*malakabee*" (a quite unprintable term of abuse, never heard in the best Peking drawing-rooms).

The afternoon dragged on till half-past four, when the second and last meal of the day arrived. Menu as for breakfast. After that I used to pass the hours by watching the Chinese troops at basket-ball on the square, or conversing in stage whispers with Farrar-Hockley and the young American corporal. As twilight gathered, the guard ordered us to lie down and sleep. Usually a cursory Chinese inspection would take place about nine o'clock, which meant torch-lights and disturbance.

That was the day from five-thirty to eight: a day of almost unrelieved monotony and boredom, with nothing to read, nothing to write with, nothing to smoke and virtually nothing to do. As a further little pleasantry, the Chinese deliberately deprived us of the issue of toilet paper. We lived in our tiny hutches unwashed, unkempt, unexercised, the realization of our increasing filthiness adding to the depression of ennui. The lack of my New Testament was a severe deprivation. You were left strictly with your thoughts, which often tended to be rather gloomy, ominous ones.

The presence of Tony next door was a great boon. I confided to him my fears about the future. "Steady on, padre," he said. "In the words of Mr. Micawber— 'something'll turn up'." Usually in the evenings, when the guards were not so vigilant, we bent down to our communication hole and carried on the most enjoyable, although sporadic, conversations. These ranged from Plato and the Book of Common Prayer to life in the airborne, and the plots of projected novels that swarmed in the Adjutant's fertile brain. Sometimes we peeped into each other's eyes, becoming absurdly convulsed with uncontrollable fits of the giggles. We grew helpless with hysterical laughter. The guard would look in, and once or twice trouble ensued, one or other of us being stood to attention to receive a dressing-down in Chinese from the guard-commander.

I used to get into conversation with the American

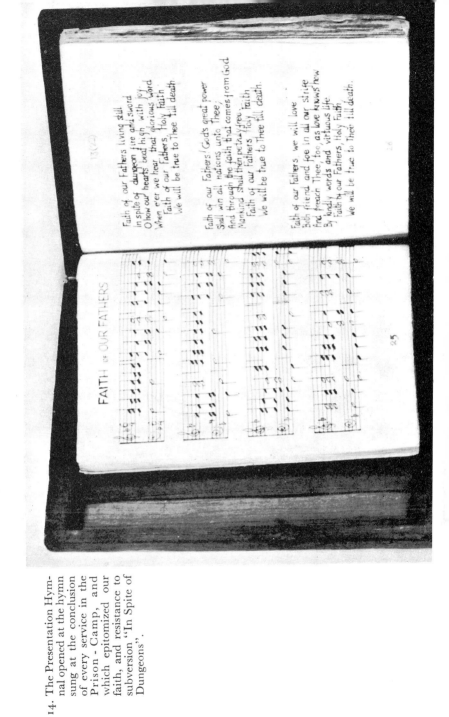

14. The Presentation Hymnal opened at the hymn sung at the conclusion of every service in the Prison - Camp, and which epitomized our faith, and resistance to subversion "In Spite of Dungeons".

The words are printed on sheets of Chinese cigarette-paper issued to us monthly. Prisoners most kindly donated sheets of their precious paper which was always at a premium.

Major Guy Ward, R.A., sewed together the sheets within an inner cover, made from cardboard and blue material from a prisoner's cotton trousers.

We had no music in the prison-camp, but Captain Deakin, of the U.S. Army, was able to transmit the tunes to paper from memory. The musical score is his work.

We had one hymn-book with us. Lieutenant Arthur Peal, of the Gloucesters, did most of the hymn-printing.

The Red Cross Society was not allowed by our Communist captors to send us supplies. It was a verboten "bourgeois, imperialist organisation". We therefore received no prayer-books, Bibles, hymnals or other ecclesiastical commodities. Everything was devotedly improvised by the prisoners.

15. The beautifully printed and illuminated prayer-book made in No. 2 Company of P.O.W. Camp 2, and presented by the prisoners to Captain James Majury, of the Royal Ulster Rifles.

(See Appendix II)

15. In No. 2 Company compound, after the camp was split and I had to remain in No. 1 Company, Captain James Majury acted as lay-chaplain.

He carried out this function with great effect, earning much gratitude from his fellow-prisoners. They presented him with this beautifully worked book as a token of regard and affection.

Lieutenant S. W. Cooper, 5th Fusiliers, did the printing, assisted by Lieutenant Arthur Peal of the Gloucesters.

The silver paper of the Cross was taken from a Christmas card from home, and the cloth cover of the book was an embroidered pillow case won by a prisoner as a prize at a camp sports meeting organized by the Chinese.

The paper throughout is Chinese-issued cigarette paper.

(Photo : Oscar Way and F. Stenlake, Colchester .

corporal, too, and give him all possible encouragement and blessing.

Abbot told me that after his capture in February, when his 'plane was shot down, he had been grilled ruthlessly to make him "confess" to the crime of waging germ warfare. He said that the first five days were the most nerve-racking experience he had ever gone through. Finding him intransigent, even in face of dire threats, the Chinese had relegated him to solitary confinement in a tiny cell under guard. They told him he was regarded as a "war criminal" who could be punished with death. When I got to know him, he had been shut away for five months without exercise or diversion. Twice a day he was fed: twice a day marched to the latrine. For the rest of the time he lay and dozed his life away. He was oppressed with the thoughts that his name might never be forwarded on the prisoner lists, and that the Chinese might never release him, even after an armistice. My presence in the adjoining cell did much to reassure him. We prayed together, and I spoke encouraging words to him through our communication hole.

Dobb and Wright, of the American Air Force, were also imprisoned nearby. Threatened with death, and even taken before a firing squad, they had not "confessed". They used to secrete, in the latrine, tiny pencilled notes containing religious phrases and exhortations to endurance, for Abbot to pick up. When Dobb was made to kneel before a Chinese interrogator, wielding a pistol, he refused to be blindfolded.

"Why?" asked the Chinese.

"Because I want to see you and pray for you to Jesus Christ."

The interrogator was completely demoralized.

Captain Dobb later gave Christian leadership in a "reactionary group" to which he was sent, and organized regular worship.

When I was released I took with me in my mind Abbot's name and address, and those of other American airmen he gave me, and safely delivered them to the senior American officer in the compound. Later, when the Chinese confronted me with the Dean of Canterbury's booklet, *I Appeal*, I longed to be able to let Dr. Hewlett Johnson know about this young corporal's testimony, and of the things concerning other officers threatened with death on account of alleged bacteriological warfare. But I was powerless, for such a letter would never have passed the Communist censors, and would have landed the corporal and me in fresh trouble.

Each night, as darkness fell, we said our prayers. I used to recite the evening prayer, "Lighten our darkness we beseech thee, O Lord", and pronounce the Blessing through the wall of each cell for the benefit of my two neighbours. Then, when we had arranged our bedding and the guard had been round, I gave three taps on each wall. This was our agreed signal for a slow, silent saying of the "Our Father". I was always aware of a profound sense of spiritual unity and peace at this time, a consciousness of the overshadowing of the Almighty in all His Love and incalculable Power. "Qui habitat in praesidio Altissimi dic Domino: Refugium meum et arx mea, Deus meus, in quo confido."

During the day, the Adjutant and I kept watch over the square and as much of the road as we could see. There was much coming and going. Sometimes "Snake-eyes" would leave by truck, carrying an important-looking brief case; sometimes the camp doctor would leave attended by medical orderlies; sometimes a high official would arrive by jeep, escorted by gunmen and saluted punctiliously on all sides. All these movements gave rise to much speculative discussion between us.

One morning, we saw that the guard with the food-buckets stopped at a disused underground air-raid shelter. Logs were drawn aside from the entrance, and a hand emerged, pathetically holding a rice-bowl. Later in the day we saw an officer wearing American flying-boots come up out of the hole. He was white and haggard, moving feebly. Returning with his guard from the latrine, he could not go down into his dank underground dungeon, but stood at the entrance gesticulating weakly. The guards shouted and prodded, until at last he disappeared into the hole and the logs were replaced.

During the next ten days, this hole had several occupants—officers we had never seen before and did not see again. These troglodytes all appeared to be in an unkempt, enfeebled and utterly despondent state. My guess is that they were American Air Force officers going through the "germ warfare treatment". It was pitiful to see the hands appearing at meal-times. We used to pray fervently for these men, that they would quickly be taken out of the pit. Eventually, they were all removed. They seemed to be taken away in the night. Later in the year the pit was filled in.

Sometimes I was taken out past the place where Major Weller lay. I would call out, "Back to back,

Sam. God bless you. Won't be long now." My guard
would chatter furiously and give me a shove. This was
a reference to the famous "Back to back" fighting
tradition and motto of the Gloucestershire Regiment,
the old 28th.

On my first Sunday in jail, August 17, I waited
anxiously for some sign that the church service was
still being held, despite my absence. I was squatting
somewhat gloomily in my cell, when suddenly the
Adjutant tapped and excitedly whispered, "Padre, there
they go. Listen." Faintly at first, and then, as the
wind veered, more and more strongly came the firm,
measured tones of "Holy, Holy, Holy, Lord God
Almighty". It was the majestic sound of some three
hundred men singing. A tremulous emotion seized
me. I could not help the tears. Praise of God filled
my soul. Despondency fell away from me. Later came
even more strongly the rousing strains of a hymn that
seemed singularly appropriate:

> "Faith of our fathers, living still
> In spite of dungeon, fire and sword.
> Oh, how our hearts beat high with joy
> Whene'er we hear that glorious Word."

It was a great morning.

Later, I learned how, to the chagrin of the Chinese,
the prisoners crowded the lecture-room to overflowing,
and made a defiant mass affirmation as a protest against
my removal from the compound. Captain James
Majury, of the Royal Ulster Rifles, was the officer
responsible for maintaining the conduct of the services,
and this he did with a reverence and dignity that com-

mended him very greatly to his brother officers, both American and British.

The Chinese authorities left me strictly alone for a fortnight. I was being left to "reflect on my crimes". On Sunday, August 24, at eight o'clock in the morning, the little hunchbacked official came for me. I was taken up to Camp H.Q. "Snake-eyes", immaculate as ever, viewed me coldly, but took no part in my interrogation. Chen Chung-Way sat at his table, smiling at me. I must have presented a barbarous appearance, unwashed and unshaven, tousled, filthy with lime and oil-stains. I knew I smelt pretty abominably. Madame Ding passed by, and her pale, pretty features contracted quizzically on seeing me. Standing there, I felt ashamed. Chen bade me sit down.

"Why you get into trouble? The Commander is very sorry to hear of your case. We did our best to warn you and help you. Why you cause trouble when we try to help you?"

Comrade Chen was shedding crocodile tears. I must admit this new approach robbed me of words.

"I hope you reflect on your mistakes, and deeply and sincerely realize your hostile attitude to us in the past."

We became embroiled in a discussion about the precise meaning of "centralization". Chen accused me of telling the prisoners it was a "new policy of *concentration*". This was absurdly untrue.

Chen summed up:

"We do not have a new policy. It is the same as always. We give full religious freedom to our prisoners and respect their beliefs. If you show repentance and criticize yourself deeply and sincerely, the Commander

say your case can be handed back to Company H.Q.,
and I think your case can be settled."

Chen was at his smoothest. As always, I asked him
about Colonel Carne.

"Do not worry. He is well. He is a free man. He
has gone to another camp."

After about an hour I was returned to my cell.

Tony Farrar-Hockley's opinion was that the Chinese
had realized the futility of their action in imprisoning
me and had determined to get me out of jail as soon
as possible, while "saving face" by extracting a "confession" and "self-criticism".

His advice was that, provided no fundamental principle
was jeopardized, I should show "repentance" and write
a "confession", putting as much into it between the
lines as I could. He said through our communication
hole:

"You are no use cooped up here, whereas as chaplain
in the compound you are of very great use. Therefore
I feel you must aim at getting back into circulation
as soon as possible."

That Sunday night, after dark, I was taken to a
Korean cottage and confronted by Tien and Liu, the
"Hatchet-man".

"We understand from Comrade Chen you wish to
repent, and confess sincerely and deeply your past
mistakes. If you do this, we can consider your case."

The next morning an incredible thing happened.
A messenger pushed pen, ink and paper through my
prison bars with a note telling me to confess. The
Adjutant and I set to work. From time to time a sym-
pathetic young olive-faced guard looked in, smiling

at me and murmuring soothingly, "Ding-how, ding-how" ("Very good, very good"). I used some of the paper for writing out several prayers and thoughts for the young corporal, and pushed them through to him.

My first attempt was considered too subtle, I think, and I was ordered to write a second "confession". This, too, was rejected. My third attempt, a couple of days later, was undertaken at night in Liu's room. I was told to write very simply and shortly, and the phrases were virtually dictated to me. I was required to state that I had "always used the religious services as a pretext for political activity". This I utterly refused to do on any account. There was an angry scene. Eventually, a compromise was reached. I "confessed" to not heeding Chinese warnings, and to "breaking the camp rules and regulations". I gave a "guarantee" that in my function as chaplain I would in the future observe the rules and regulations. I was immensely surprised when Tien told me that I had even violated the rules laid down for P.O.W. religious leaders in the Geneva Convention. I was surprised, because this was the first time the notorious "bourgeois" Geneva Convention had come into it!

Liu gave me a long speech couched in Marxian dialectical phraseology. He told me I had set a bad example as a priest, but that as I had shown signs of repentance and had confessed, I was to be given "lenient treatment". My sentence was one month's solitary confinement. I felt reasonably happy—at least I *knew* my fate. This would mean a total of six weeks and four days. (Our Chinese captors never reckoned the waiting period before sentence. Sometimes a man was kept five weeks in jail, and *then* given three months

solitary.)   Liu went on to say that my sentence was
to be suspended and that I would be returned to the
compound that night:

"We shall watch your conduct.   If you break your
guarantee we shall carry out this suspended sentence
against you."

I was taken back to collect my few belongings from
my evil-smelling cell, and then Tien accompanied me,
in the darkness, back into the compound. As we walked
through the village, he said, quite pleasantly:

"I think you have learnt very much."

I replied:

"Yes, Tien, I have indeed."

My fellow-prisoners were preparing for sleep as I
came in.   Even so, I received a heart-warming, enthusi-
astic welcome.   I dumped my foul clothes, and, late
as it was, a hot swill-down was prepared for me by the
kitchen staff.   The date was August 28.   I was back.
It seemed like a minor liberation. The Armistice could
wait!

16. Presentation page of the Hymnal carved and hand - printed by prisoners in Camp 2.

16. After P.O.W. Camp 2 was split into two companies, in compounds separated by about a mile and a half, the Chinese authorities allowed me to pay two visits in seven months to the new compound to celebrate Holy Communion.

After the Easter service there in 1953, the prisoners presented me with this hymnal. No other presentation which I may be fortunate to receive in later life could equal it in value. It is a unique treasure.

Lieutenant S. W. Cooper, 5th Fusiliers, did the hand-printing on this page.

CHAPTER ELEVEN

The Final Phase

By comparison with the cramped, filthy conditions of the jail-cell, life in the compound seemed spacious and good. At this time, September, 1952, the Chinese reduced the perimeter of the compound and greatly strengthened the fencing and wire. I was rash enough, a few days after my release, to touch the fencing in the course of a meditative stroll. With much excited shouting, the guard took me to Tien. I was stood to attention to await the Chinese Company Commander's pleasure. For this meaningless "crime" I was submitted to an extraordinary interrogation lasting about half an hour.

"Why did you touch the fence?"

"I don't really know. I assure you it was a perfectly innocent action."

"We do not believe you. Every action has a motive. What was your hidden motive?"

This seemed to me the limit of absurdity.

"We think you wanted to test the strength of the new fence. Are you planning to escape?"

"No, and if I *was* do you think I would openly test your fence in broad daylight within a few feet of your guard?"

"Do not tell the Company Commander. He knows all about the case. He knows you have a hidden motive."

The same old brick wall: heads only got hurt. I gave up, finally being let off with a severe reprimand.

I had brought back from the cell some important messages from Tony Farrar-Hockley to members of the compound. It was a great pleasure to see him released about twelve days later. The American corporal I did not see until just outside Panmunjom in 1953, while we awaited release. He returned safely to the States, and has been given a decoration for gallantry.

My New Testament, taken from me when I was thrown in jail, had not been returned. Several times I went to Tien and worried him for it. He was sulky and would give no co-operation. Finally, I spoke to Chen Chung-Way about it. A week later he personally returned the little Bible, and got me to sign a receipt. He inquired after my welfare and gave me a warning to "be good". It sounded almost too trite. I had been released from jail on August 28. It was September 27 before I got my Testament back, after repeated requests.

From mid-September onwards the Chinese opened a big campaign to convince us of the truth of their claims that the U.N. were waging bacteriological warfare in Korea and Manchuria. Day after day I was taken to Tien's house with some five or six others, and given a couple of hours on it. We were asked to read newspaper articles on the subject, and statements said to have been made by captured American Air Force officers. At these sessions, cigarettes would be handed round, tea and sweets sometimes offered, and we would be assured that we were not going to be "forced" to believe anything. The idea was to "awaken our consciences" by "revealing the truth" to us. We were asked leading questions like "Do you admit germ warfare is a horrible crime against humanity?" or "Do you know that America refuses to ratify the Geneva Protocol against germ warfare?"

A well-arranged photograph exhibition was organized. Squad by squad we were taken to see this, and invited to express our opinion "freely". We saw photos of dead rats, dead fish and dead foxes, all said to have been dropped, heavily infected with plague and cholera, from U.N. 'planes over Korea. We saw Chinese doctors gingerly picking up flies, spiders and other "deliberately infected" pests from snowy fields, and placing them in bottles for laboratory investigation in Peking. We saw pictures of germ canisters supposed to have been dropped, and photostat copies of the explicit, signed confessions of captured American "germ warfare criminals".

A good deal of this visual propaganda seemed to us pathetically unconvincing or "rigged". A more sinister manifestation was the tape-recorder machine playing back conversations between Mrs. Monica Felton (Great Britain) and American Air Force officers, who, in strong terms, "confessed" their share in "a crime against the peace-loving people of the world", and expressed their loathing of this terrible weapon of the "warmongering, imperialist, capitalist clique".

One morning, after a night of heavy air activity, we found some silver radar-ribbon strewn about the compound. Our Chinese were in a ferment. A medical squad cordoned off the "danger area", and the ribbon was carefully picked up with tweezers and placed in bottles. An American called out: "Aw, come on, doc. Columbus took a chance!" We were vastly amused to see the orderlies going about this work with hands and wrists liberally iodine-ized, and wearing protective face masks.   A Puerto Rican officer, watched by a horrified group of Chinese, nonchalantly wrapped a piece of the silver ribbon round his neck like a tie.

The Chinese had earlier informed me of the Dean of Canterbury's visit to China.   One night I was summoned to H.Q.   A pamphlet by the Dean, entitled *I Appeal*, was placed before me.   It was a statement against the alleged use by the U.N. of germ warfare in Korea and across the Chinese border.   The Dean seemed convinced by things he had been shown and people he had interviewed that this was so.   The Chinese told me that he was one of the "very few" Church leaders who was morally brave enough to obey his conscience in this matter.   They said:

"He is a true Christian.   His conscience impelled him.   What about you?   You are also a Christian chaplain.   We hope your conscience will awaken you and that you will act in a righteous way."

I remained entirely non-committal.   They also showed pictures of Russian Orthodox prelates speaking at anti-germ warfare rallies, and statements by them. I was confronted by impressive lists of Chinese Anglican and Roman Bishops, and Protestant religious leaders in China, who were signatories to condemnatory statements and appeals against the alleged use of the bacteriological weapon.   I was shown photos of nuns in procession in Shanghai and Peking, carrying slogans against germ warfare.

"Do you think these Christian leaders are for or against the peace-loving peoples of the world?"

We were being flooded, at this time, with verbal

and written agitation against germ warfare. Perhaps the Chinese had their greatest triumph when Colonel Schwable of the American Marine Air Corps "confessed", and stated over Peking radio that his "eyes had been opened", and that he now saw, for the first time in his life, the issues confronting humanity.

To me it was interesting to observe the reaction among the prisoners-of-war. When our captors had first commenced the campaign way back in March, 1952, there was sheer unbelief and ribald amusement.

This was followed later in the year by a more serious consideration by most officers of the whole question. There was prolonged discussion. Almost everyone agreed that "the Chinese can get you to confess to anything if they are determined to", and that "confession under duress" was obviously valueless.

Later still, among the American officers mostly, an apologetic note began to creep in. "Well, I suppose our side knows what it's doing", and "I bet the Russians and Chinese are going to use it anyway", or "After all, if it *is* being used, there must be a good reason, and anyway is it any worse than the atomic bomb?" A more unconcealed attitude emerged in some: "Anything's good enough for these . . . . . . .s. If we use it well, hell, I'm all for it."

On October 16, 1952, the Chinese suddenly and without warning split P.O.W. Camp 2 into two separate compounds. About one hundred and eighty officers, British and American, were marched down the road to their new home about a mile away. We had been hauling logs and carrying clay all summer for the new buildings.

I just had time to entrust Colonel Carne's stone

cross to a young Gloucester subaltern for use in the new compound, and to hand over a few of our home-made hymn books and a New Testament. In my compound we retained the large, majestic wooden crucifix carved by an American Marine officer.

It was a sad blow. Many tried comradeships were broken by the separation. We felt, too, more exposed to Chinese methods now that our erstwhile formidable solidarity had been reduced. For days after the split, the old compound seemed like a "camp of ghosts". I very soon appealed to the Chinese for permission to visit the "Church of the exile" every Sunday for religious ministrations. I received a scornful "No". Sun asked me:

"Do you think we have to send a chaplain to all our prisoner-of-war camps?"

Both compounds made a strong appeal for a Christmas visit, and to this the Chinese finally consented. For days I could get no definite verdict from them, right up to the last desperate moment. Then, half an hour before the proposed Christmas service, Chen Chung-Way personally took me to the new compound. I had already celebrated Holy Communion for my own people.

It was moving to see old comrades again in their new surroundings. They had turned their camp library into a homely little chapel, adorned with a skilfully made lectern and prayer-desk, the work of an American major. On the altar stood a newly-made cross and candlesticks. These had been made by the British. Sheets of rice-paper with a simple religious device in coloured crayon were stretched from leg to leg of the altar table, giving the effect of a white frontal.

The choral standard was amazingly good. An American officer was responsible for this, with a mixed British-American choir. I conducted Christmas morning service at eleven o'clock and preached. Afterwards I celebrated Holy Communion. The Chinese gave me time to have a mug of tea and a pasty with the British community, for I was fasting. At one o'clock Chen took me down the road to the old compound. Naturally, I carried with me many messages of greeting. That night we had a Carol Service and an impromptu concert.

Captain James Majury, of the Royal Ulster Rifles, was acting as "lay-chaplain" in the new compound. He maintained a high standard of worship there in my absence, and gave fine religious leadership. Many profited from this, and as a mark of esteem his fellow-prisoners printed for him an exquisite book of prayers with illuminated capitals.

Again, on Easter Sunday, 1953, I was taken by Chen to visit the new compound at eleven in the morning. I preached at the Easter Service and celebrated the Easter Mass in my prisoner's uniform, using the tin cup for chalice and Major Ryan's wooden paten. At the end of the Easter Service I was greatly moved when a formal presentation was made to me on behalf of the new compound. I was given a hymn-book printed by the prisoners on sheets of Chinese cigarette-paper, and bound inside a beautifully-carved wooden cover with hinges made of tin from old cans. It was the workmanship of five American and British officers. I still have it, a treasure for a lifetime. The inscription reads:

Presented to
The Reverend S. J. Davies, B.A., C.F.
Chaplain to the Church of the Captivity
by
The Members of his Congregation
in
No. 2 Company
Prisoner of War Camp No. 2
North Korea
EASTER SUNDAY
April 5th, 1953

One day during this last year in Camp 2, some of the prisoners saw Ding's little daughter come through the compound, in the care of her guardian, playing with a small gold box a little larger than a toilet compact. Several who had been in Camp 5 in the grim old days recognized it. It was Father Kapaun's Communion pyx, or ciborium. A delegation of prisoners sought an interview. Finally, Comrade Sun, on behalf of the Chinese Commander, called for the American Roman Catholic leader and assured him that at the proper time this "dead man's property" would be entrusted to him. This promise was fulfilled, and the ciborium went back to the States after the Armistice—the relic of a Saint.

Soon after New Year, I began to write a version partly from memory, partly improvised, of Bernard Shaw's *Pygmalion*. Max Nicolls, a subaltern of the Royal Ulster Rifles, with a deep literary and theatrical interest, helped me, also creating a "Colonel Barclay", played by Major Paul Docker. We produced a version

17. Church Service, March 1953.
An original sketch done in No. 2 Company Compound, P.O.W. Camp 2, by
Major Guy Ward, T.D., R.A.

18. Prisoners at Volley-Ball, Camp 2.
An original coloured sketch by Major Guy Ward, T.D., R.A., dated August 1952.

17. The date of this sketch is significant—March 1953. It explains why chairs and long wooden benches with back rests appear. Until February of this year, the year of release, we enjoyed no such things. Suddenly, they began to be provided by our captors. We guessed a prisoner-exchange was in the air.

This room is the camp library. It is still cold, and the prisoners are wearing their padded blue winter jackets.

In the sketch, the mixed American-British choir are grouped under their choral conductor to the right of the altar.

The Cross and candlesticks were made by the British; the lectern by an American Major, Duke Slater.

The Chinese consistently evaded our request for a complete Bible for the lectern.

Before leaving for Panmunjom, the prisoners burnt most of the church equipment.

18. The building is the thatched kitchen. Behind can be seen the steeply-rising mountains that enclosed the camp. The scene is sketched from the raised promenade running along the front of the Korean schoolhouse in which we lived.

Some prisoners are wearing under-pants only, others blue cotton trousers. Both were supplied by the Chinese.

The temperature is about 95°, hence the players are stripped to the waist.

The Chinese themselves were keen volley-ball players, and supplied us with net and ball. American enthusiasm for the game soon spread to the British, with whom it is not so well known.

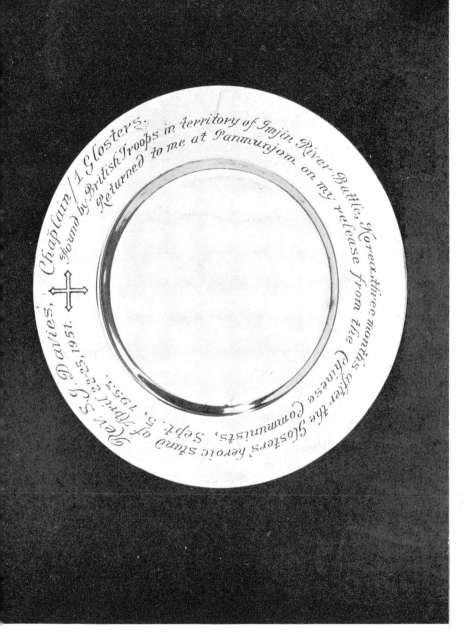

19. My Communion Paten, lost during the Battle of the Imjin. Its story is inscribed round the rim (by Boodle and Dunthorne, the Silversmiths, at Liverpool)

19. Within half-an-hour of my release, on September 5th, 1953, the British Senior Chaplain returned to me this little field-service paten. He told me its story: "One day, just after our re-capture of the lost Imjin territory, a patrol was crossing a paddy-field when one of the soldiers noticed the rim of something shining in the mud. He picked it up, and cleaned away the dirt. He saw the inscribed cross. 'This looks likes a church plate,' he said. They took it back with them to the padre. Immediately, of course, he identified it as a paten. We knew it could only belong to the Gloucesters' chaplain: to you. So here it is. Rather a nice little welcome-home present."

On my return to England, I had it polished up and inscribed. It was consecrated, along with a new chalice, by the Bishop of Stepney, and is in use again at the celebration of Holy Communion.

under the title *Rain in Spain*, which enjoyed a tremendous success among the prisoners. "Dolittle" seemed to me likely to incur Chinese suspicions of an insult to the working-class, so I rechristened Eliza and her engaging father "Turnpenny". For the benefit of our American audience I introduced a visitor from the States, Elmer J. Brooker, into the hilarious tea-party scene, and also threw in a somewhat asinine Kensington vicar with an ear-trumpet. This prompted me to interpolate the rather inevitable exchange:

> *Cynthia Bassington-Bowker* (played by Max): "I hear you don't drink tea in America, Mr. Brooker.
> *Elmer*: "Well, that's not strictly true. Of course, we mostly drink coffee, but many people do drink tea.
> *Vicar*: "After all, my dear, they *did* have a tea-party, you know. At Boston, eh, Brooker—ha, ha, ha.
> *Freddie Bassington-Bowker*: "Oh, jolly good, vicar, jolly good."

This sally brought our American cousins enthusiastically to their feet at all four performances.

Alan, a young Gloucester subaltern, achieved an outstanding success as Eliza. I played the part of Professor Higgins. Again with an eye for our audience, I introduced an "aitches" lesson:

> "In IDAHO the housewives hourly hurry home with heads held high."

At the tea-party, Eliza gravely trotted this out with devastating effect.

The play was superbly produced by Max and other

helpers in appallingly difficult conditions. Our "props" consisted of laths, a few sheets of cardboard, many copies of the London *Daily Worker* and *Shanghai News*, and paint. The Chinese gave us pins, grease-paint, and a few pieces of sheeting and silk. With this unpromising material Robin, of the Royal Ulster Rifles, Bob, of the U.S. Air Force, and their small team worked what must be called "wonders".

On May 4 in this last year of captivity, the famous "Camp Rules and Regulations" were displayed for the first time on a large board, signed by Wang Yang-Kung. There was ironic cheering. Thus it was that only four months before release "rules" for violation of which men had been severely punished, were at last made known!

The religious services continued in accordance with the Chinese "policy of centralization", and were still censored at H.Q. I appealed for an Ash Wednesday service, but no reply was vouchsafed. I held the service, and was later called to H.Q. and reprimanded. I also appealed for a service to commemorate Coronation Day. Permission was refused and I was warned not to "organize". We said our prayers together secretly on Coronation Night, at the remarkable feast organized in one of the squad-rooms, complete with invitation cards, little flags, candles, a superb "gateau Westminster" and potato whisky. That is a story in itself.

Paul Docker, acting Senior British Officer in the absence of Major Weller, who had been "collected" by the Chinese at 5 a.m. on June 1 and placed in solitary, greeted the representative group of captive American officers; called on me to say the State prayers for Her Majesty from the Book of Common Prayer; and then led us in a hearty singing of the National Anthem. We divided the huge cake, made unbelievably "from nothing" by the kitchen staff, and toasted the Queen in "Vin Pomme de terre".

Suddenly we were aware of the presence of Comrade Sun. A silence fell on the candle-lit room. He gazed without expression upon the flags, the cake, the framed newspaper portrait of our lovely young Sovereign Lady, which someone had received through the post. From the background a voice chanted:

> "The people's flag is deepest pink
> It hangs above the kitchen sink . . ."

Sun went. We decided to round off our party, which had been a great success, and go while the going was good.

In a few moments Sun was back with reinforcements. He grabbed at the flags; someone whisked away to safety the Queen's portrait; others knocked back the potato-hooch and consumed the remnants of the cake, or threw chunks to the Americans now crowding the top of the room-partition, cheering, shouting and hurling their vehement "sonofabitches". Sun demanded the platter on which the Coronation cake had rested. It now contained only a few crumbs. With this he attempted to reach the door, elbowed from all sides. Outside in the darkness, whistles were blowing and Chinese guards came running. Against my better judgment I shouted:

"Sun, you have offered to the British people to-night an insult we shall not forget."

There was for a moment a tricky silence.

"The people," he screamed, "the people! You are

not the people, you are the imperialist, reactionary, ruling clique, the enemies of the people."

"Nonsense," I said, "You are a stupid man, and I refuse to listen to you."

Paul Docker tactfully bade me to silence, and attempted to push Sun as gently as possible through the crowded door. As soon as the Chinese had left, Paul and I raced to our sleeping-quarters, hastily pulling on all possible clothing, for we fully expected to be lying in the cold, dismal cells before midnight. Everyone else thought so, too.

To our surprise, nothing happened. I spent a wakeful night on my wooden bunk, listening apprehensively to every footstep. I was amazed to be still a "free man" next morning. That day, Peking radio announced that Chou-En-Lai had sent Winston Churchill a telegram of greeting to commemorate the Coronation. We heard no more of it in our prison camp, nor did the Chinese take any reprisals against us for our clandestine celebrations.

Big events were the death of Stalin, which the Chinese observed with much solemn mourning; the Rosenberg trial; the accession of Malenkov; the more conciliatory tone of Molotov and the alarming behaviour of President Syngman Rhee.

In the day-time men did their chores and washed their clothes; played cards and chess; exercised on the hard, baked square, and sat in the shade talking wistfully of everything from cubism to the love of women. It was supremely a time for "remembrance of things past". We lived on memories, and a man with a good, racy story from the old days was a popular guest.

In the warm night, under the white moon we paced

our compound, while the bull-frogs roared from the paddy-fields, and on occasion the timeless majesty of Beethoven's Fifth or the "Eroica" swept over us from the "squawk-boxes" high up in the trees. And all the time, beyond the conversation of the moment your mind was asking "Shall I get home, will it all end— when, where, how?" Then the Chinese whistles blew. We went slowly to our dim squad-rooms and our straw mats, with a last sad look at the moon, shining there like a silver shilling in the vast sky—fairies' moon, lovers' moon, bombers' moon.

CHAPTER TWELVE

Yu-Ti

CHINESE children have a charming custom at the New Year. It is believed that at this time the household "lares et penates" make their annual report to Yu-Ti, the God of Heaven. In order to give them a favourable last impression and to prevent them saying unwelcome things, the children make much of the household images, burning candles and paper money before them and sealing their mouths with sweet, sticky candy.

During the last six months of the captivity our Chinese captors made tremendous improvements in our daily life. For the first time we got sleeping bunks, chairs and tables. Razor sets, mirrors, combs, nail-clippers, toilet-bags, tailor-made cigarettes, wine and beer— all were issued. We began to get meat. A favourite American question became: "Whad'ya think of Communism now, comrade?" The answer remained the same: "Not much."

The Chinese knew the Armistice was in the offing and that their prisoners were going home. Was it, I wonder, "a case of Yu-Ti"?

Soccer was played almost daily by the British, and this year the Chinese even provided gaily-coloured stockings and jerseys. The Americans continued untiringly with baseball. A crack Negro team was allowed to visit the camp, and some wonderfully skilled baseball and basket-ball was seen. In memory I see the dusty square alive with the playing men, and hear with nostalgic clarity the rippling American chatter:

"Hey there, baby, baby, baby. Whad'ya say, babe, whad'ya say?"

"Now whad'ya gonna do, barrer, barrer, barrer?" (batter).

"Stay loose, Colonel baby, stay loose."

"Now then, big team, whad'ya say, whad'ya say?"

"Easy man now: easy man."

The biggest surprise of all was the Camp Olympics: eight days of jumping and track-running with every help from the Chinese. Our little track measured two hundred and two yards. To this meet came a group of British other-rank "reactionaries"—another surprise concession by our captors. We guessed things were folding up at Panmunjom. I had to face a good deal of Chinese unwillingness and sarcasm to get permission for these visitors to attend Sunday service. I was asked, quite bitterly:

"Why do these men come here?"

"To take part in athletics."

"Yes, they have not come here to join in religious services."

Eventually, after delaying our accustomed worship for nearly two hours, the Chinese sulkily gave way and allowed them to attend.

I was able to give much religious help to this group, and wrote out prayers and Bible readings for them to use in their own camp. I also drew up a short commemoration service for Coronation Day, which they took back and used. In their camp a group of "ultra-reactionaries" were still imprisoned in tiny cells. Men of the calibre of Corporals Hartigan, Upjohn, Holden and Matthews, and private soldiers like Godden, Godwin, Haines and Kinne had existed for months in "the kennels", four and a half feet by two and a half. I wrote a message to these men, concluding with the noble text:

"Great is TRUTH and it shall prevail."

I have since learned it was smuggled to the men and read by them all, giving comfort and help in their adversity. Corporal Smith and Corporal Bailey, both Gloucesters, gave great assistance in these matters, the latter doing much to organize religious worship in his compound.

One afternoon we suddenly heard pistol-shots. "Snake-eyes" came rushing through our compound, hatless, with his long black hair streaming in the wind. A gunman followed him. More shots. We were on fire with curiosity. Was he being liquidated by the Party, or escaping from Chiang Kai-Shek assassins? Chinese began swarming over the hillside. We saw a limp body being carried down. There was much coming and going. An orderly came through the compound carrying Ding's hat.

That night we harried our interpreters at roll-call. At last Tien said: "A deviationist adventurer try to kill Commander. He has now been accounted for." We thought so, too. It had certainly been an incident in the classic tradition. It was good to know that even "Snake-eyes" had his little troubles.

Manual work continued. We used to march under guard nearly four miles to the Yalu River to unload

20. The Cross from Korea is handed over to the Dean for safe-keeping in Gloucester Cathedral, at the Gloucesters' great Thanksgiving Service, November 21st, 1953.

From left to right : Rev. S. J. Davies, M.B.E., C.F.; the Dean of Gloucester, the Very Rev. Seiriol J. A. Evans, M.A., F.S.A.; the Adjutant, Captain Anthony Farrar-Hockley, D.S.O., M.C.; the Commander of "B" Company, Major Denis Harding, D.S.O.; the R.S.M., Mr. Hobbs, M.B.E.

20. The climax of the service was the handing-over of the little stone cross, symbol of endurance and redemption.

It now rests within the Cathedral, adjacent to the Gloucesters' Memorial Chapel. The accompanying inscription reads:—

THIS CROSS WAS MADE
DURING HIS CAPTIVITY
BY
Lieutenant Colonel J. P. Carne, V.C., D.S.O.
who commanded the 1st Battalion
THE GLOUCESTERSHIRE REGIMENT (28th-61st)
AT THE
BATTLE OF THE IMJIN RIVER
22nd–25th April 1951
and was used at the religious services
held in the prisoner of war camp.
Pyn-chong-ni North Korea.
1951–1953.

(Photo : Copyright "Gloucestershire Newspapers Ltd.").

barges, and haul logs. We enjoyed the walk in the sun and the disarming illusion of freedom it gave. At the reservoir, the Chinese allowed us to swim at mid-day. This was sheer delight: cool, green water on hot, tired limbs; cloud-puffed blue; the jagged mountains rising steeply; thoughts of English seas and beaches, English rivers, sun-soaked lawns, home.

We now had a complete Shakespeare in the library, and I spent many hours in the cool, beautiful after-dawns learning the sonnets by heart.

The camp library, while still retaining its predominantly Marxist character, now included a certain number of novels, allowed by the Chinese as "progressive", and therefore suitable reading for "tools of the imperialist warmongers". Such were *Les Misérables; David Copperfield; Tess of the d'Urbervilles; The Last Frontier* by Howard Fast; *War and Peace*, and Sholokov's magnificent *Quiet Flows the Don*. We always had a fair number of Soviet novels in English translation. These tended to deify rather cardboard-like figures labelled "Soviet man" and "Soviet woman", who were model workers. Among these, Maxim Gorky's works stood out in a class by themselves. His *Childhood* and *The Artamanovs* impressed me deeply as major works of art.

With pathetic hopefulness we noted the days on which no air-activity was heard. If we reached three such days a feverish excitement used to mount. Could it mean the peace we all longed for? Our rising hopes were always dashed by a flight of jets high above the camp, leaving their long white trails in the cloudless blue.

The sick had been exchanged. Peking Radio's English broadcasts, relayed into the compound, although shrouded with a fog of ambiguity and often full of question-begging propaganda, were tending to betray optimism. Even Syngman Rhee's activities seemed less dangerous. An Armistice was in the air—in our blood.

One sunny July morning word spread that Commander Ding was to address the camp that afternoon. The optimists said, "This is it"; the pessimists said: "Russia's probably come in."

At two o'clock we assembled on the square. Everyone was tense, looking straight ahead. At least it was a diversion. The Commander, the same immaculate, sauntering "Snake-eyes" of old, came across the square with interpreter Wong, who looked rather smugly non-committal. Gunmen escorted them. All the Chinese camp staff were present.

Commander Ding spoke in Chinese. A pause, pregnant with unimaginable possibilities, and then Wong spoke:

"Both sides in the Korean war have agreed to a cease-fire to take effect from . . ."

A hundred and eighty hearts thumped again. No one moved; no one spoke. The Chinese cameramen were poised ready for snaps of the "joyful prisoners hailing the great victory of the peace-loving people at Panmunjom." They were disappointed. Ding and Wong finished. We broke up and walked away like men in a dream, up the steps and into our billets. No one cheered or laughed. The time was too great to grasp.

Next morning we held a great Service of Thanksgiving. Very many were there. I preached to the camp. I took as my theme the healing of the ten lepers.

In their adversity they cried "Have mercy", but, their troubles over, only one turned back to give thanks.

"What about you? In the prison camp, when hope seemed dead, you turned to God. Soon you're going home. It will be easy to forget Him. Are you going to be numbered with the nine who forgot to give thanks?"

I appealed to the Chinese for wine for a Thanksgiving Holy Communion. They were as obstructive as ever. They gave a half promise. Finally I was called over the following Sunday an hour after the service had been due to start. Two bottles of wine stood on the table. Tien said:

"We give you the wine."

I said:

"I am sorry, but the men have gone away to breakfast. It is too late. Perhaps to-morrow or next Sunday."

Tien followed with:

"You must write out in detail word for word the Communion Service."

I said:

"This is a new rule. You did not ask for this before."

He was obdurate.

"Write it out word for word for the Commander's approval."

"Very well, Tien, in that case we shall not have our service. Good morning."

I left him sitting there with the two bottles of wine. The compound supported my action. Censorship of this kind was like a red rag to a bull for everyone. Men felt they could wait now till release.

Major Weller had been thrown into jail once more just before the Armistice, falsely accused again of "inciting to subvert the Camp Authority". They feared his wide influence and courage. He would not "confess" to anything, and the Chinese were furious about his case. Threats of "no release" were being hurled about.

We were all at this time being summoned to H.Q. for individual interviews pending our release. I was summoned. I criticized them very severely for their action over Major Weller, and warned them that the U.N. would never countenance the detention of senior officers on such charges. Liu and Tien were beside themselves with anger.

"Watch your conduct. You are one of the trouble-makers in the camp. You still have a suspended sentence. We can carry this out and you will not be released. Self-consciously watch your behaviour."

It was rather disturbing, but somehow one felt these were pygmy threats.

After a thorough "shake-down" we were prepared to leave for Panmunjom. Colonel Carne suddenly reappeared. His reserve seemed very great at first. Everyone wanted to shake his hand, to speak to him, to crowd round him. He was obviously unused to company after his long time in solitary, but he acted towards all, regardless of rank, with a kindly forbearance and patience that must have cost a great effort. Soon one began to be aware again of his characteristic dry humour. His presence with us seemed a symbol of immense reassurance.

On August 19, in pouring rain, we left by truck for the railhead. We travelled in cattle waggons to Kaesong —a two-day journey full of discomfort and inconvenience. But what did it matter? We were going home.

We remained for endless days under canvas in the

Chinese transit camp near Kaesong, living on beans
and rice, beans and rice. Groups began to depart
every other evening after nightfall. Those of us left
behind grew restive and sleepless. Boredom and uneasy
surmise took their toll. Each day seemed a year. In
the twilight we used to gather in groups, sitting on the
Korean burial-mounds, watching the yellow moon push
up over the mountain crest.

Each Sunday I conducted service in the eating-hut.
Our thankfulness was aptly summarized in Psalm 126:
"When the Lord turned again the captivity of Sion,
Then were we like unto them that dream."

The British numbers dwindled to a very small group.
I was in it. Even Colonel Carne had been released,
and Majors Harding and Weller. When the Chinese
called out "Carne" on the list one evening, there was
a large outburst of clapping and cheering from the
Americans. This was a moving tribute in spontaneity
and frankness.

I could not help noticing that in the last group still
left were all those who had played a big part in the
religious activities—Major Ryan, Captain Majury,
Lieutenant Nardella (the American Roman Catholic
leader) and myself. Coincidence or policy—who knows?

On September 5 I was released. Very early that
morning we underwent a further shake-down. I was
allowed to keep religious articles. Little hunchbacked
Chen Chung-Way sidled up. His scarred face split
into his old smile. The filmy eyes swam. His head
jerked as he said, somewhat superfluously, but not
unkindly:

"So you go home now?"

"Yes, Chen, I go home now."

It was not a brilliant conversation. Chen did not offer his hand. I am glad he didn't, although had he done so I believe I would have taken it. It is hard to refuse that most human of gestures, which speaks of man's desire for brotherhood and understanding.

Before we embarked on the Chinese trucks for the exchange point, our captors had a last fling. We received a doubtless sincerely-meant exhortation to enlist in the battle for peace, with the peace-loving peoples of the world against the warmongering imperialists, who were enmeshing the people in a web of lies, and preparing to unleash a new world war. We knew it by heart.

Behind the Chinese stood several European Red Cross observer-delegates. A bronzed, bush-hatted Australian was there, grinning broadly. We had just heard that England had won the Ashes. As the Chinese speaker droned on, Drum-Major Buss of the Gloucesters ("old Drummie") called out:

"Who said the Aussies can play cricket?"

Comrade Sun glared impotently at the tall, smiling Englishman.

THE END

APPENDIX I

"A Cross From Korea"

MEMORIES OF A PRISON CAMP

To the Editor of The Times

SIR,—On Saturday, November 21, during the Gloucestershire Regiment's thanksgiving service in Gloucester Cathedral, the Dean and Chapter will receive into their keeping from the 1st Battalion a small, beautifully carved cross made from grey Korean stone. It is a Celtic cross, because its maker is a Cornishman. For all who were with Colonel Carne during the stirring times in which he won the Victoria Cross, and were later with him in P.O.W. Camp 2, North Korea, this little stone symbol is a treasured thing.

Colonel Carne carved it in captivity using only a couple of nails and a primitive hammer, and I have a vivid recollection of him during the bitter December weather of 1951 patiently, day after day, rubbing smooth the sides of the cross on the concrete steps of the Korean schoolhouse in which we were imprisoned. He presented it to me for use in our religious services, and it first graced our crude altar that Christmas at the Holy Communion in the drab camp lecture-room, the temperature below zero, with the portraits of Marx, Lenin, Stalin, Mao Tse-tung, and the rest gazing down.

It was at this service, the first Eucharist of the five we were able to celebrate during two and a half years, that Colonel Carne made his first and last Communion of his captivity, for he was taken from us on January 28, 1952, and after his "trial" by the Chinese Communists went into the long period of solitary confinement which did not end until we saw him again three weeks after the Armistice this year. At this service our chalice was a Chinese metal cup, our paten a British mess-tin. Vestments I had none. But we had the essential matter —wine, bread, a pocket Book of Common Prayer, and the intention to consecrate and offer the Eucharist in accordance with the rites of the Holy Church. More than 100 British and American officers received the Sacrament. I was not allowed to visit the other ranks.

Colonel Carne's cross stands some 10in. high, rising sturdily from its rough-hewn plinth. The arms of the cross, at the top of their small column, are embraced, after the manner of a Cornish cross, by a circle of stone. When Colonel Carne was invested recently by Her Majesty with his great award, there were those of us who were thinking also of this other cross, so patiently and so beautifully carved under somewhat bizarre circumstances. In my prayer of blessing of this cross in the prison camp these words occurred: "May all who look to it with faith and love be given grace to endure unto the end." Now, in Gloucester Cathedral, this sturdy symbol of redemption and endurance carved from Korean stone, will find, it is our hope, a resting place for centuries to come.

Yours obediently,

S. J. DAVIES, Chaplain,

1st Bn., the Gloucestershire Regiment.

November 18, 1953.

The above letter appeared in "The Times" of November 20 and is reprinted by permission of the Editor.

APPENDIX II

A Book of Selected Prayers

SOME NOTES FROM CAPTAIN J. H. S. MAJURY

This book contains a selection of the Prayers used in the religious services held in No. 2 Camp Annex, Prisoner of War Camp, North Korea, during the period from October, 1952, to September, 1953. As there was no padre in this camp, I conducted the services. The book was printed and bound in prison camp by two British officers—Lieutenant S. W. Cooper (The Leicestershire Regiment, attached The Northumberland Fusiliers) did the actual printing, and Lieutenant Arthur Peel (The Gloucestershire Regiment) did the designs.

Under the conditions of religious intolerance practised by the Chinese, the compilation of this book was not an easy task. The material on which to work was extremely limited. The paper used was that issued to us with which to roll cigarettes, a cheap, rough paper on which writing was a problem in itself. The lettering was done with an ordinary pen nib, the designs and illuminated capitals were done with a few coloured crayons which were acquired. The book was sewn with an ordinary needle and thread, the stiff back was one removed from a Communist propaganda novel! The printing was done in secret during August, 1953, shortly before the prisoners-of-war were released. It was presented to me by the members of our "Church" on the last Sunday in that camp, before we finally moved south to be repatriated. During the printing of the book the Chinese discovered it and took it away, suspecting it to be something sinister and subversive. It was only reclaimed after a long argument with the Chinese administration of the camp, in which they were persuaded that it was merely a selection of prayers and not a secret method of taking "reactionary" propaganda out with us.

The book was again removed from me the day we left our camp for the journey south. After reading the first few prayers to a Chinese interpreter who could barely interpret—he decided it was too much for him, and anyway he was too tired after carrying out a search of our kit all afternoon—and so with the remark "I think this very good work, but oh dear, so much trouble," he resignedly handed the book back to me!

The book contains some of the loveliest prayers in the Prayer Book, all ones which fitted the circumstances under which we lived. Only our Prayer of Thanksgiving, which I composed for our service on the day we were told the Armistice had been signed, is included at the back of the book in my own handwriting.

In my mind the book is a standing testimonial of the part religion played in upholding our morale and the trouble men took to put their faith before anything in face of the severest opposition.

(*Signed*) J. H. S. MAJURY

APPENDIX III

A SERMON—

Preached on Christmas Day, 1952
at No. 2 Coy. Compound,
P.O.W. Camp 2, North Korea

It was taken down in shorthand by a listener,
brought out of captivity, and a copy sent from
the United States

. . .

St. John 1 : 14—*"And the Word was made flesh, and
dwelt among us."*

"To-day the Christian world is united in celebrating
once again the Festival of Our Divine Redeemer's birth.
In this commemoration, barriers of space and time are
done away, and Christians everywhere feel their unseen
bond of faith and prayer—the holy worship centring
upon the Infant Christ and the Blessed Mother in the
stable at Bethlehem. All over Christendom the bells are
ringing; the old carols are being sung; and heart speaks
to heart in spontaneous joy. It is primarily a family
festival; a time for reunion; for home-comings; for the
children; for the giving of presents—all this is essentially in
honour of the Holy Family, in thanksgiving for the gift of
Christmas, CHRIST HIMSELF. 'And the Word was made
flesh, and dwelt among us; and we beheld his glory, the

glory as of the only begotten of the Father, full of grace and truth.'

For us Prisoners of War the great Festival has a particular poignancy, and to-day especially, our thoughts are with our families in our beloved Motherlands. We are united spiritually with them, and they with us. Is not that a wonderful thing—something calculated to inspire and strengthen us? The knowledge that we are being prayed for—that God, the source of all Power, all Love and Truth is watching over us in all our dangers and necessities: that his purpose for each one of us runs through our lives like a thread, whatever might befall us. . . .

As we recall the Christmas scene so familiar to us and so dear since childhood—the Christ Child in the manger; the Holy Mother; St. Joseph, and the shepherds—we remind ourselves of the very core of our faith. What is it? It is that God Himself became man. The Divine Power entered into human history in the person of JESUS of Nazareth, the child of Bethlehem. God took our human nature upon Him, and lived as man among us men, experiencing our human joys and sorrows; our troubles and difficulties, and lastly, death itself. Christ took our human nature and our flesh in order to redeem it; to tell us the way, the truth and the life in human language that all can understand. 'I am,' he said, 'the Way, the Truth, and the Life'; and 'I am come that they might have life, and that they might have it more abundantly'. *There* is the core of our religion. As we say in the ancient words of the Nicene Creed—'Who for us men and for our salvation came down from Heaven, and was incarnate by the Holy Ghost of the Virgin Mary, and was made man.' Recently I was reading these words by a critic of the great nineteenth century novelist, Dostoevsky: 'He was one of ourselves, a man of our blood and our bone, but one who has suffered and has seen so much more deeply than we, that his insight impresses us as wisdom . . . that wisdom of the heart that we seek that we may learn from it how to live.' And I thought—isn't that overwhelmingly true of our Saviour Himself? JESUS CHRIST our Lord, truly God, yet also truly man—Eternal Wisdom, the Word of God made flesh.

In a few moments we shall be receiving Holy Communion. Under the outward form of bread and wine we shall receive, as food of the soul, the Body and Blood of our Lord, once offered for us upon the Cross. As though with Christ in the upper room at Jerusalem we partake with the apostles of the Last Supper, obeying by our action the Master's command: 'Do this in remembrance of me.' In the Blessed Sacrament we unite ourselves with the Lord, that we 'May dwell in Him and He in us.' By our devout reception of the Sacrament we cleave to Him that we may share in His Joy, in His Peace, in His Love, in His triumph over sin and death. It is the pledge of our immortality, the token in this life of Eternal Life. Instead of a golden chalice we shall drink from a tin cup. Instead of from a gold or silver paten we shall receive the Bread of Life from a rough wooden platter. Strangely fitting! Our Saviour was born in a stable and laid in a manger. Perhaps we shall always remember these few Communions in the prison camp as among our most precious experiences. 'Faith, our outward sense befriending, Makes the inward vision clear.'

The message of the Church to us at Christmastide is one of peace and joy. The Peace of Christ is something we can possess in our hearts even though outward circumstances speak only of war and disruption. Christ's Peace is internal—think of his words to the disciples: 'Peace I leave with you, my peace I give unto you—not as the world giveth give I unto you'. St. Paul in the New Testament speaks of 'Peace in believing', and in one of our familiar prayers at Evensong we pray that God will give to us 'That peace which the world cannot give'. When the surface of the ocean is lashed to fury by a great storm; when the waves roar and toss: in the depths there is peace, and all is still. So, even in the midst of outward turmoil, the Christian can be at peace in the depths of his being. Let me quote from an eighth century Greek hymn—

'Jesu, deliverer, near to us be;
Soothe thou my voyaging over life's sea:
Thou, when the storm of death
Roars, sweeping by,
Whisper, O Truth of Truth,
"Peace, it is I." '

To-day we stand at Bethlehem, looking into the future. What does it hold for us? We do not know, and it is well that we don't. 1953 looms ahead like an enigma. One thing is sure. Each one of us is in the hand of God, and *we are called upon to fulfil at all times our vocation as Christian men in this particular set of circumstances.* It is not easy, Christ never promised that it would be. His own life on earth was not easy, and he attained his victory only through suffering. But if we ask, God will give us all that we need: to endure, and not to falter. He will give us rich gifts of patience, good humour, forbearance, courage, faith, hope and perfect charity. Our religion does not promise us escape from suffering and trial, but it does promise us the God-given power to endure to the end,

and to triumph over all 'the slings and arrows of out-
rageous fortune' with calmness, dignity, and sublime trust.
A great French preacher once declaimed to a congregation of men in a notable sermon at Notre Dame, Paris—
'Men, for the love of God, be men.' Let us take that for
our motto in 1953, and God will surely 'crown His gifts
with strength to persevere.'·

I thought for a long time what message I could finally
leave with you were I permitted to visit your camp this
Christmas. I found the answer in St. Paul's Epistle to
the Colossians (2, 5-7):

'Though I be absent in the flesh yet am I with you in
the spirit, joyfully beholding your order and the
steadfastness of your faith in Christ.

As ye have therefore received Christ Jesus the Lord,
so walk ye in Him.

Rooted and built up in Him and stablished in the
faith as ye have been taught, abounding therein with
thanksgiving.' "

Half-an-hour later, I was taken back by Chen
Chung-Way, to No. 1 Coy. Compound, just over
a mile down the road, and did not return until
Easter Sunday, 1953.